T0089251

# My Big Activity Book

BuzzPop

Give the octopus eight legs!

**Connect the dots to reveal a beautiful insect!**

Spot the three differences in this scene!

Answers on page 190

**Match each number with the correct group of fruit!**

Answers on page 190

**Draw a picture of yourself!**
**There's no one else in the world like you.**
**You're special!**

Castles are gorgeous!

Decorate the birthday cake!

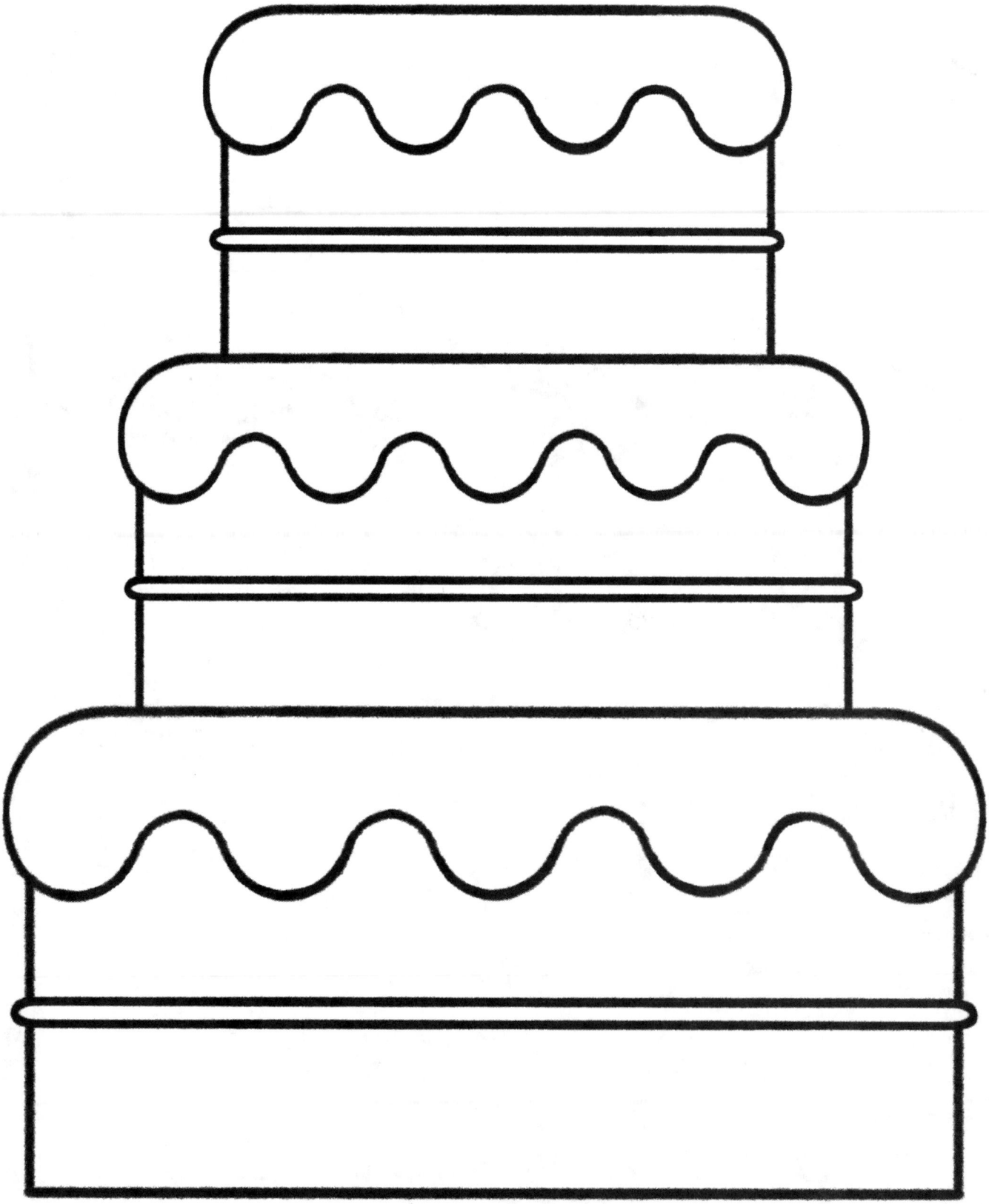

**Ahoy there! Add four flags to this pirate ship!**

Can you find the group of four frogs?

Answer: C

**Connect the dots to reveal something you ride!**

## Can you match each of these leaves?

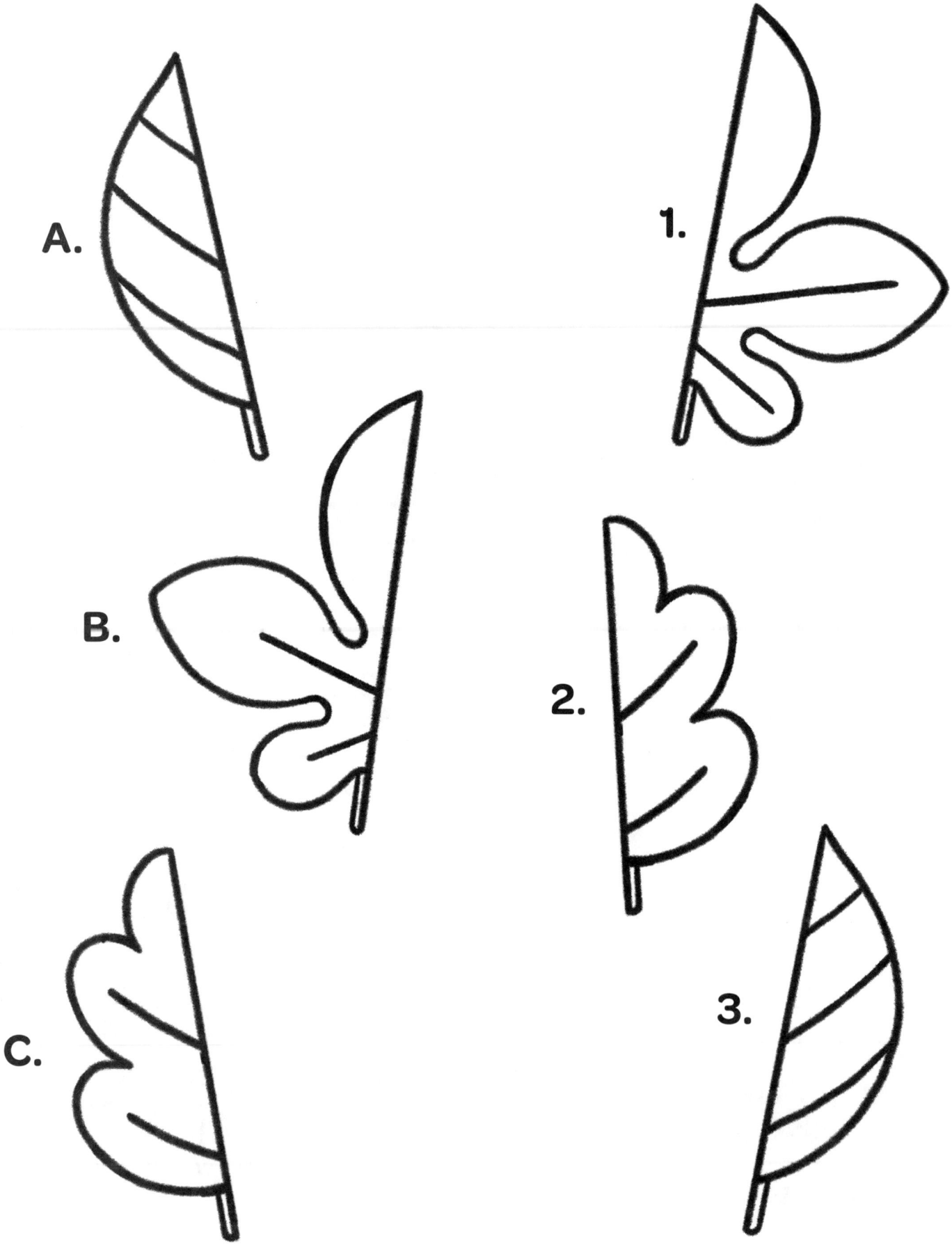


Answer: A-3, B-1, C-2

There are a lot of fish in the sea!
Draw a fish you'd like to find.

**A shark's sense of smell is 10,000 times better than a human's!**

Tigers pounce at night.
Add five stripes to this big cat!

***Brrr!*** **Decorate this snowman.**
**Make sure he doesn't get too warm!**

Sports can be a lot of fun!

**Practice your shapes!**
**Draw some circles!**

***Meow!*** **Can you help get the kitten to her yarn?**

Answer: B

What has two tires and two pedals?
Connect the dots to find out!
14
15
12
11
13
16
10
4
5
3
2
7
6
8
1
20
9
17
18
19

**Spot the three differences in this scene!**

Answers on page 190

Match each animal to its name!

CHICKEN

SHEEP

MOUSE



Answers on page 190

**The sky is clear!**
**Draw an airplane flying through the air.**

***Whoosh!*** **Draw yourself in the sailboat.**

**What's your favorite pizza topping?**
**Add yours on the pizza below!**

**Bats come out at dusk.**
**Draw two bats flying through the sky!**

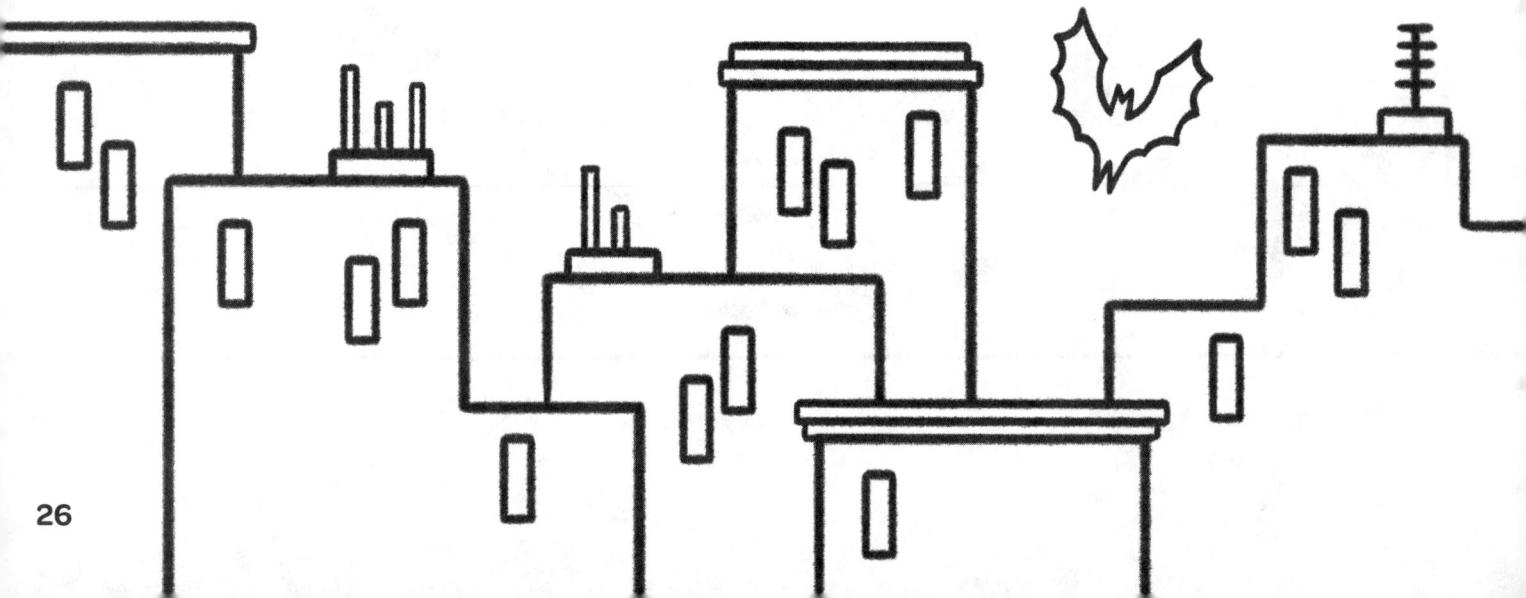

## Finish the patterns!

Answers on page 190

Look, a lucky ladybug!
Color the shell red and the spots black.

Answers on page 190

**Connect the dots to reveal something you eat for dinner!**

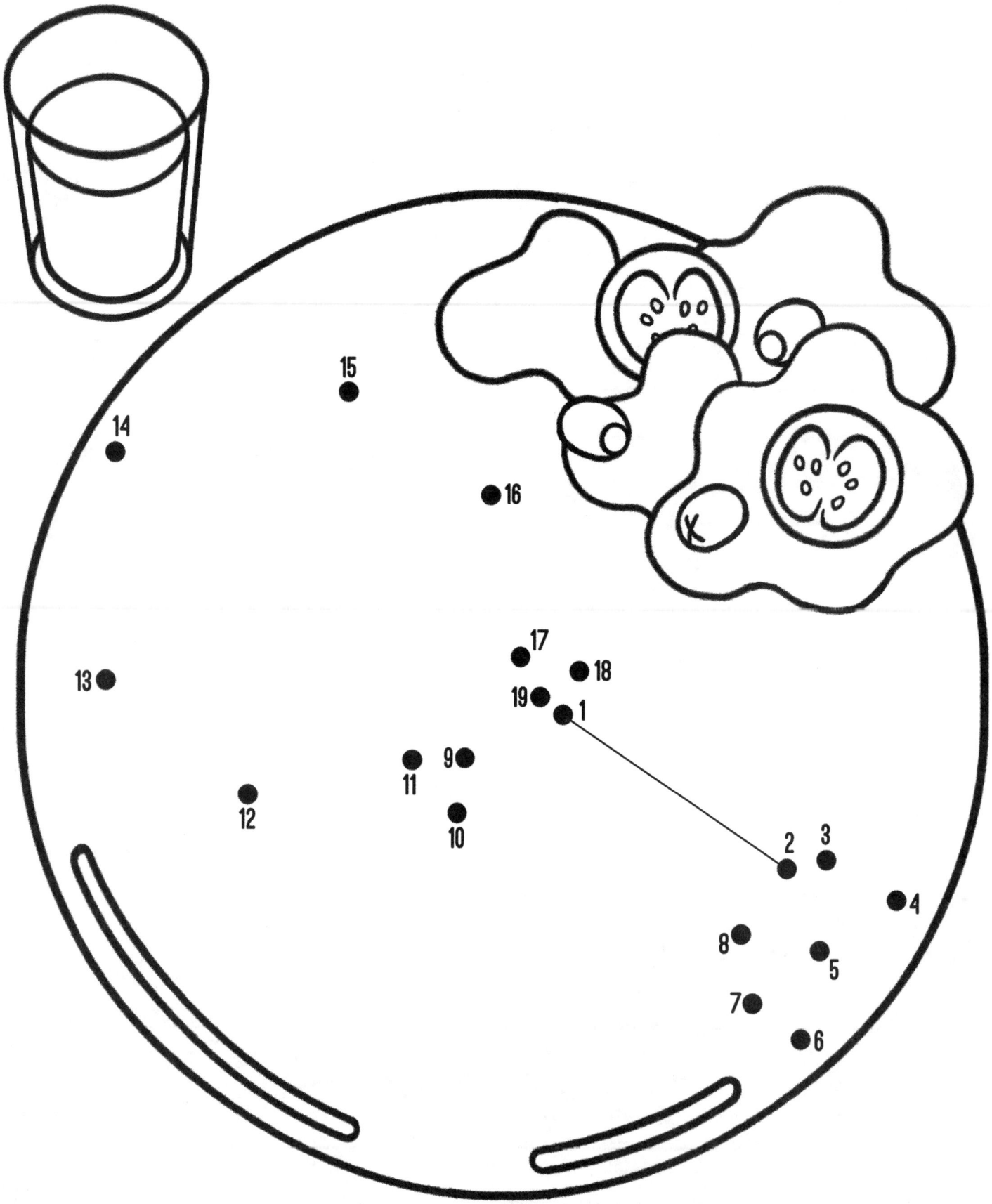

**Spot the three differences in this scene!**

Answers on page 190

Can you match each vegetable to its color?

GREEN

ORANGE

PURPLE



Answers on page 190

*Vroom!* Draw a car.

Did you know that dolphins have two stomachs?

**Decorate the gingerbread cookie!**

This umbrella blocks the sun.
Add a beach towel and a beach ball!

**Connect the snake's head to its tail with some wavy lines!**

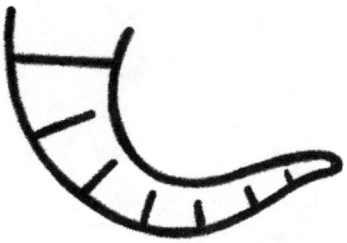

Circle the group of six fireflies!

Answer: B

***Tweet! Tweet!*** **Draw a path from the bird to the nest.**

Answers on page 190

**This bird has flippers, not wings. Do you know what it is?**
**Connect the dots to find out!**

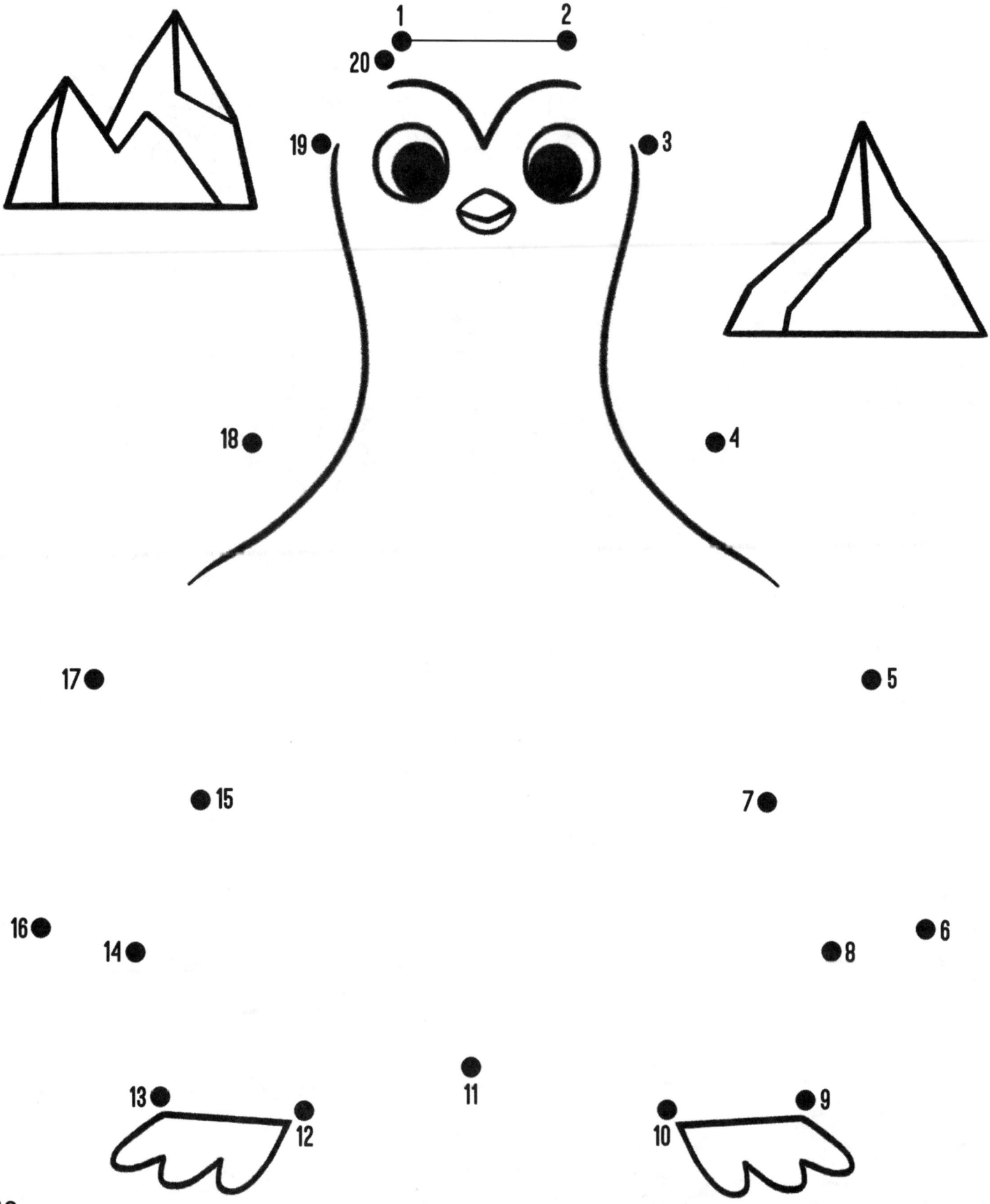

**Spot the three differences in this scene!**

Answers on page 190

**Match the snacks below!**
**What is your favorite snack?**

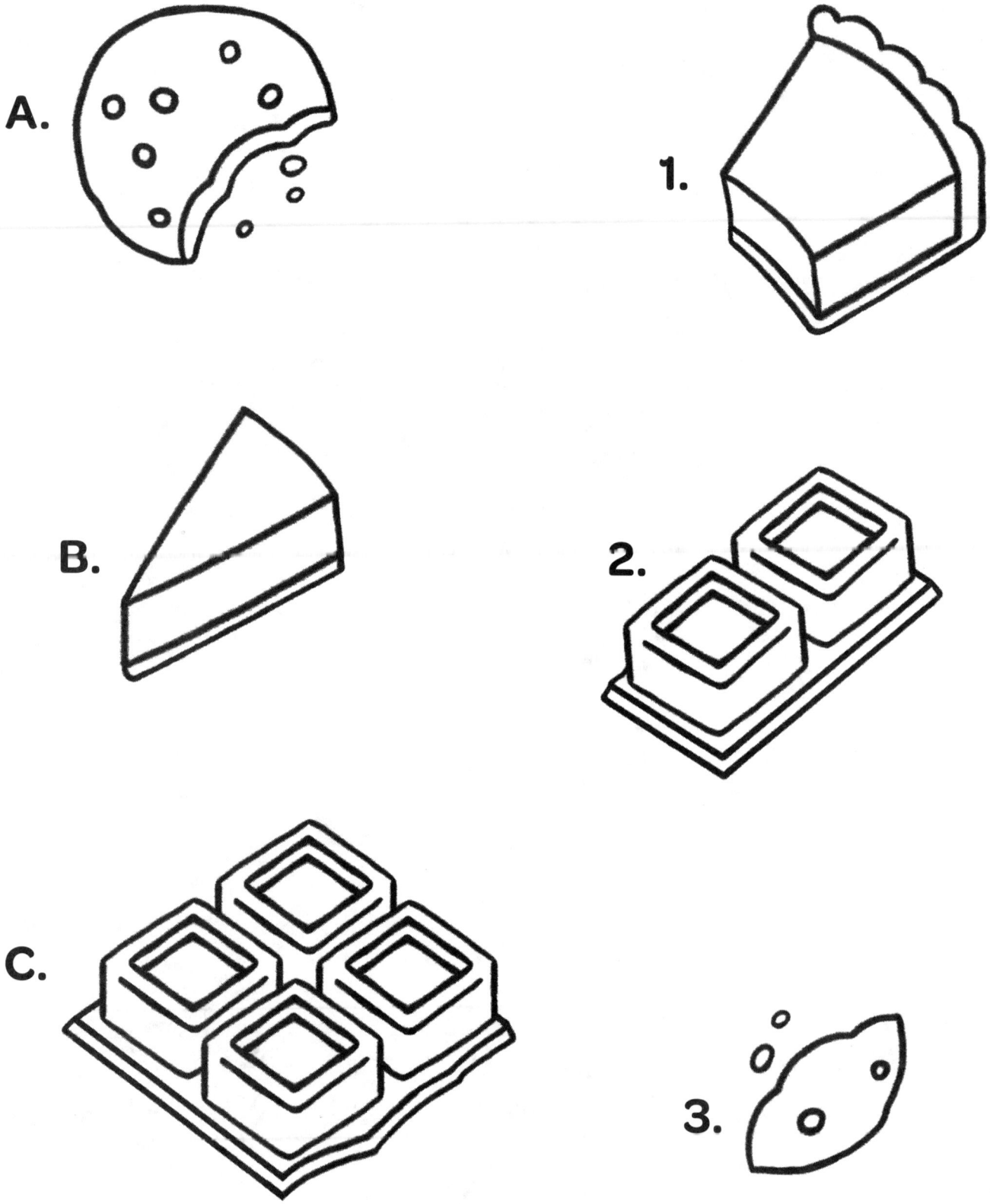


Answer: A-3, B-1, C-2

**Enjoy a day on the lake!**
**Draw a boat.**

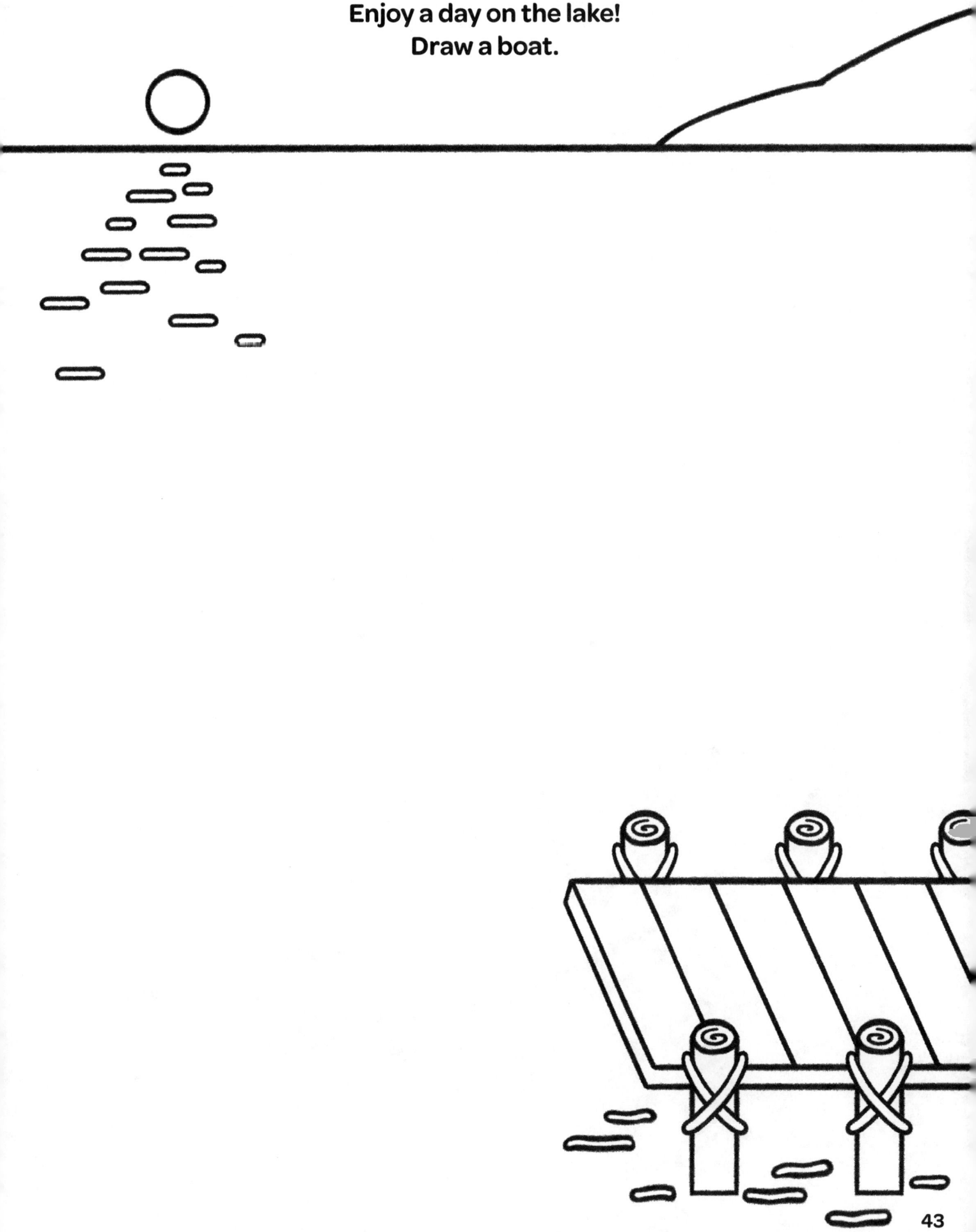

Watermelon is a sweet snack in the summer!

**Do you like ice cream?**
**Cover this sundae with your favorite toppings!**

***La, la, la!*** **Mermaids love to sing!**
**Can you draw two mermaids sitting on this rock?**

## Finish the patterns!

Answers on page 190

**Practice your shapes!**
**Draw some triangles!**

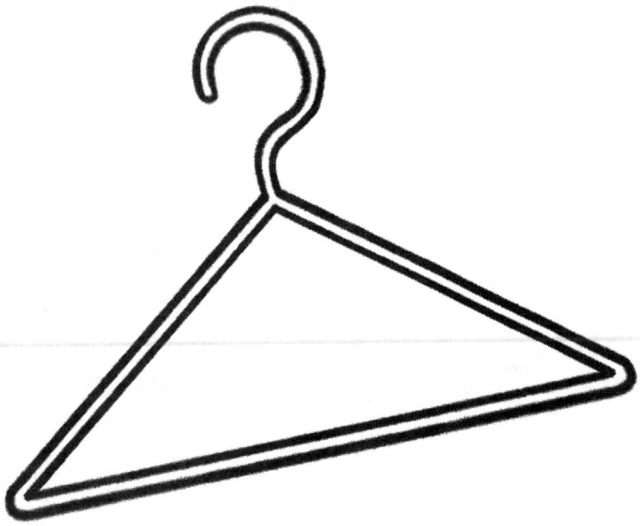

***Roar!*** **Draw a path through the rocks and grass to help the dinosaur find her friends!**

Answers on page 190

Connect the dots to complete this umbrella!
It'll keep you from getting wet.
12
11
13
10
14
9
15
7
5
20
19
17
8
6
4
1
18
16
3
2

**Spot the three differences in this scene!**

Answers on page 190

Match the shape with its name!

SQUARE

STAR

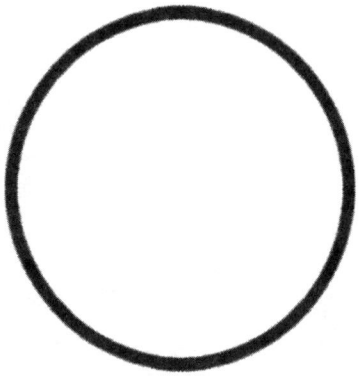

CIRCLE

TRIANGLE



Answers on page 190

**Draw your own planet!**
**Is it round? What color is it?**

Ice-cream cones are a sweet treat!

**What color would you like your bike to be?**
**Color it in below!**

The caterpillar looks hungry!
Draw an apple hanging from the tree.

***Buzz! Buzz!*** **Draw a busy bee!**

Circle the group that has only one beach ball!

Answer: C

***Blast off!*** **Can you help the astronaut get to her space shuttle?**

Answers on page 190

These can live for thousands of years!
Connect the dots to find out what it is.

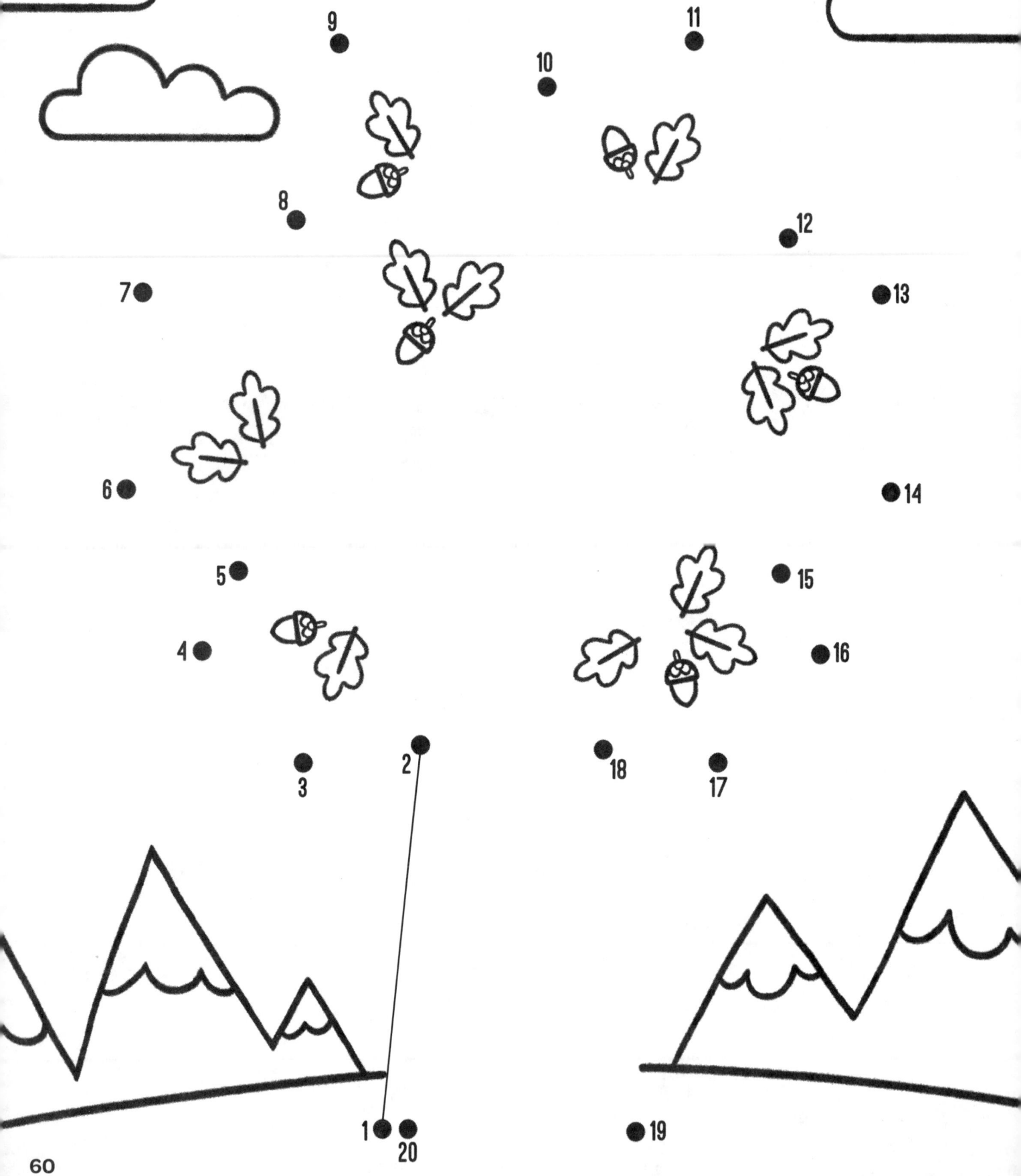

**Spot the three differences in this scene!**

Answers on page 190

**Do you like puzzles?**
**Match the puzzle pieces below!**

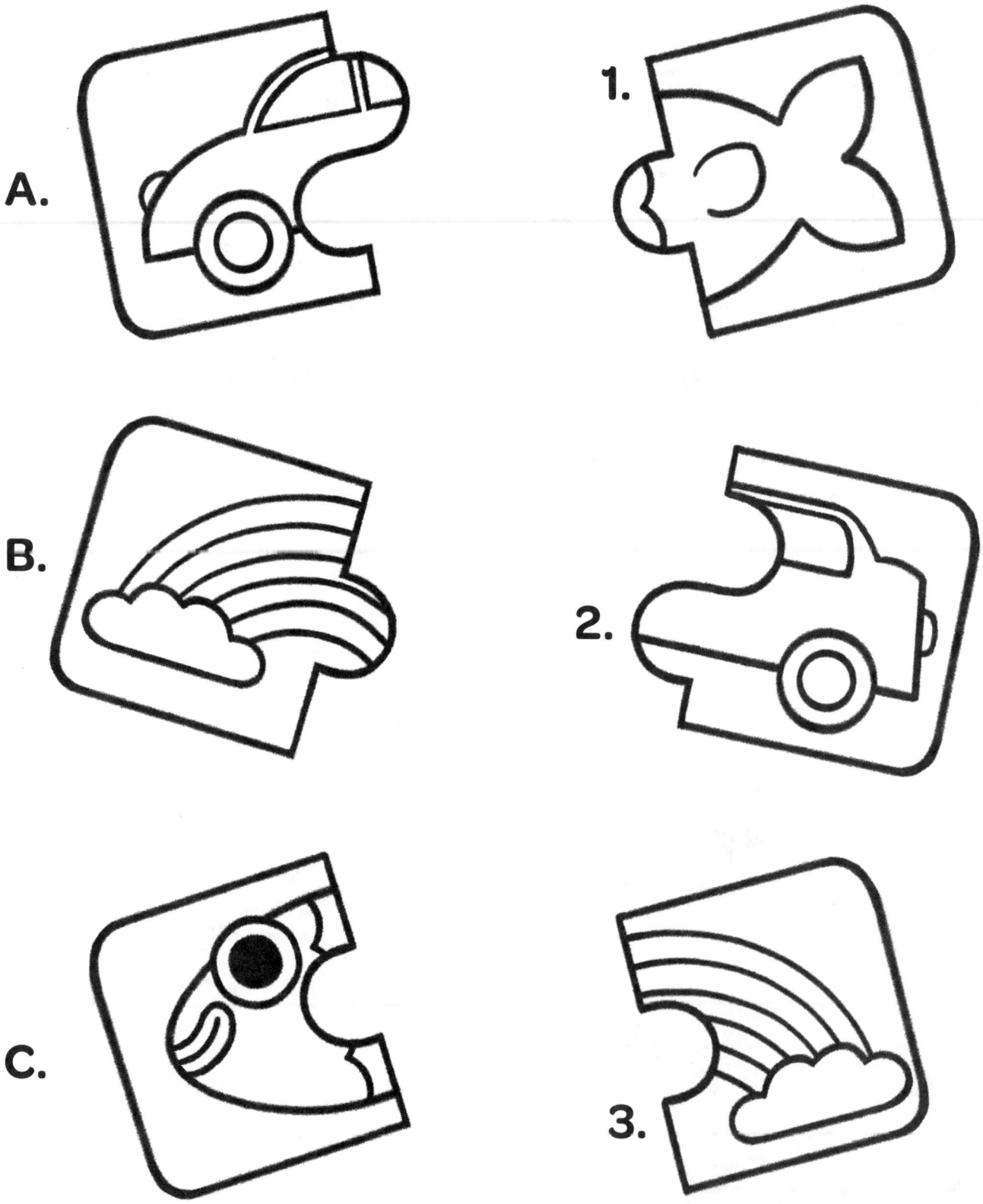




Answer: A-2, B-3, C-1

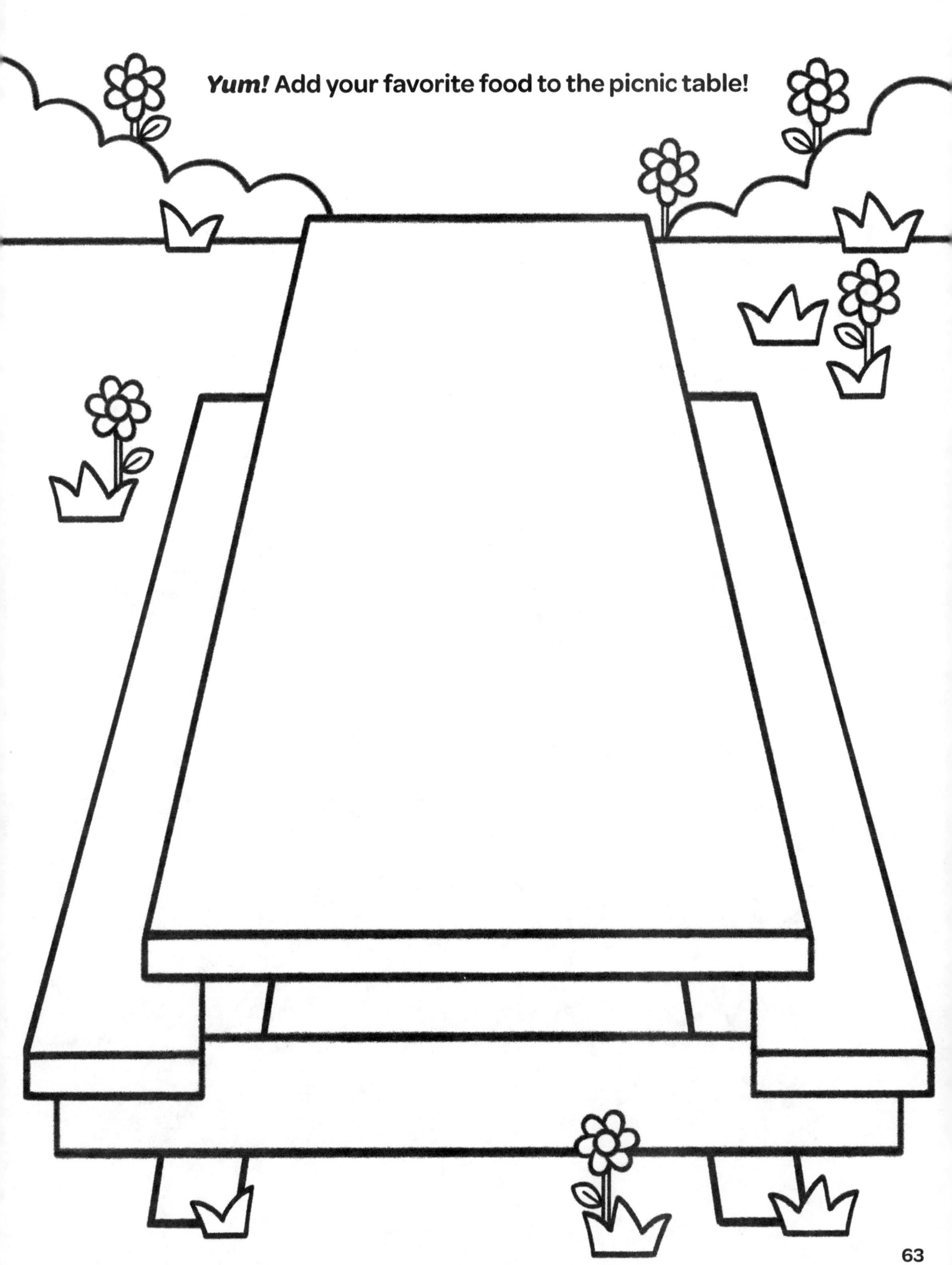
*Yum!* Add your favorite food to the picnic table!

Flamingo chicks are gray when they hatch!

Dogs are the best!
Decorate this doghouse.

***Moo!*** **Add five spots to the cow.**

Can you find the group of three kittens?

Answer: C

## Finish the patterns!

Answers on page 190

Dancing is fun!
Can you help the dancer get to their ballet slippers?
A.
B.
C.
D

Answer: B

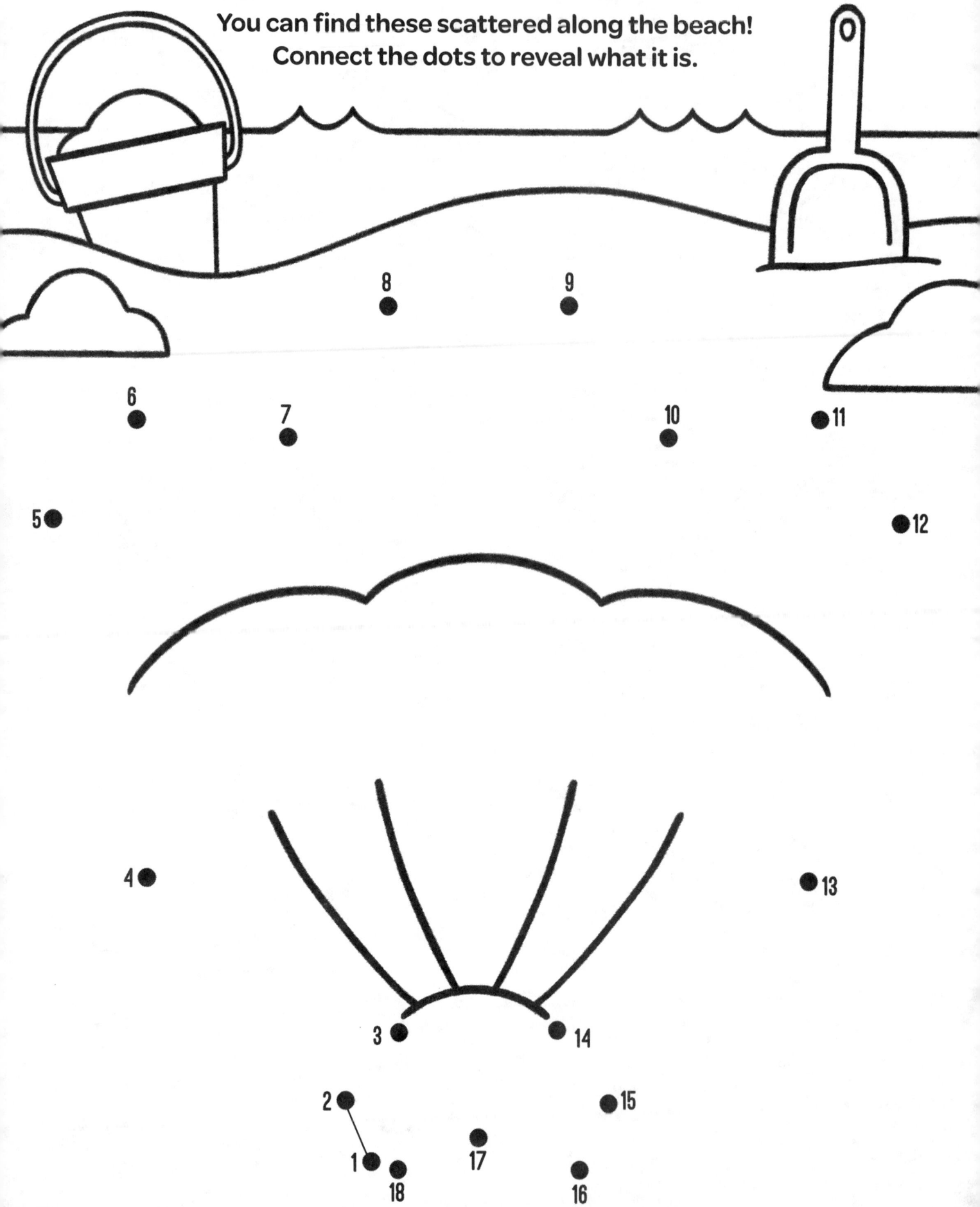
You can find these scattered along the beach!
Connect the dots to reveal what it is.
8
9
6
7
10
11
5
12
4
13
3
14
2
15
1
17
18
16

Spot the three differences in this scene!

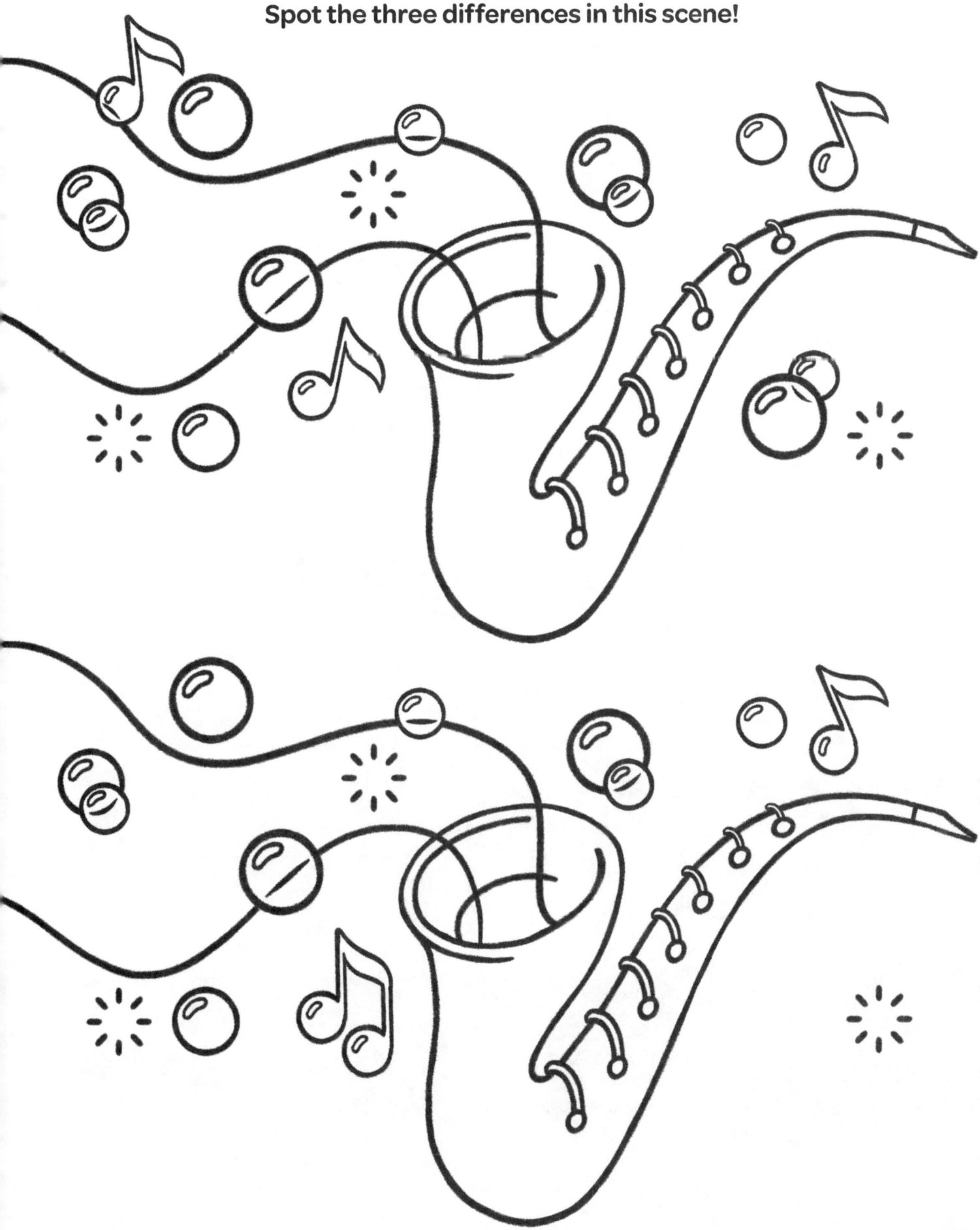

Answers on page 191

## Can you match each animal to its home?

A.

B.

C.

D.

1.

2.

3.

4.

Answer: A-4, B-3, C-1, D-2

Did you know jellyfish don't have brains?
Add some jellyfish to the water!

It's a lovely day at the beach!

**Lizards love the heat!**
**Color in the sunbathing lizard.**

It's snack time!
Add two of your favorite cookies to the plate.

**Find the group of five eggs!**

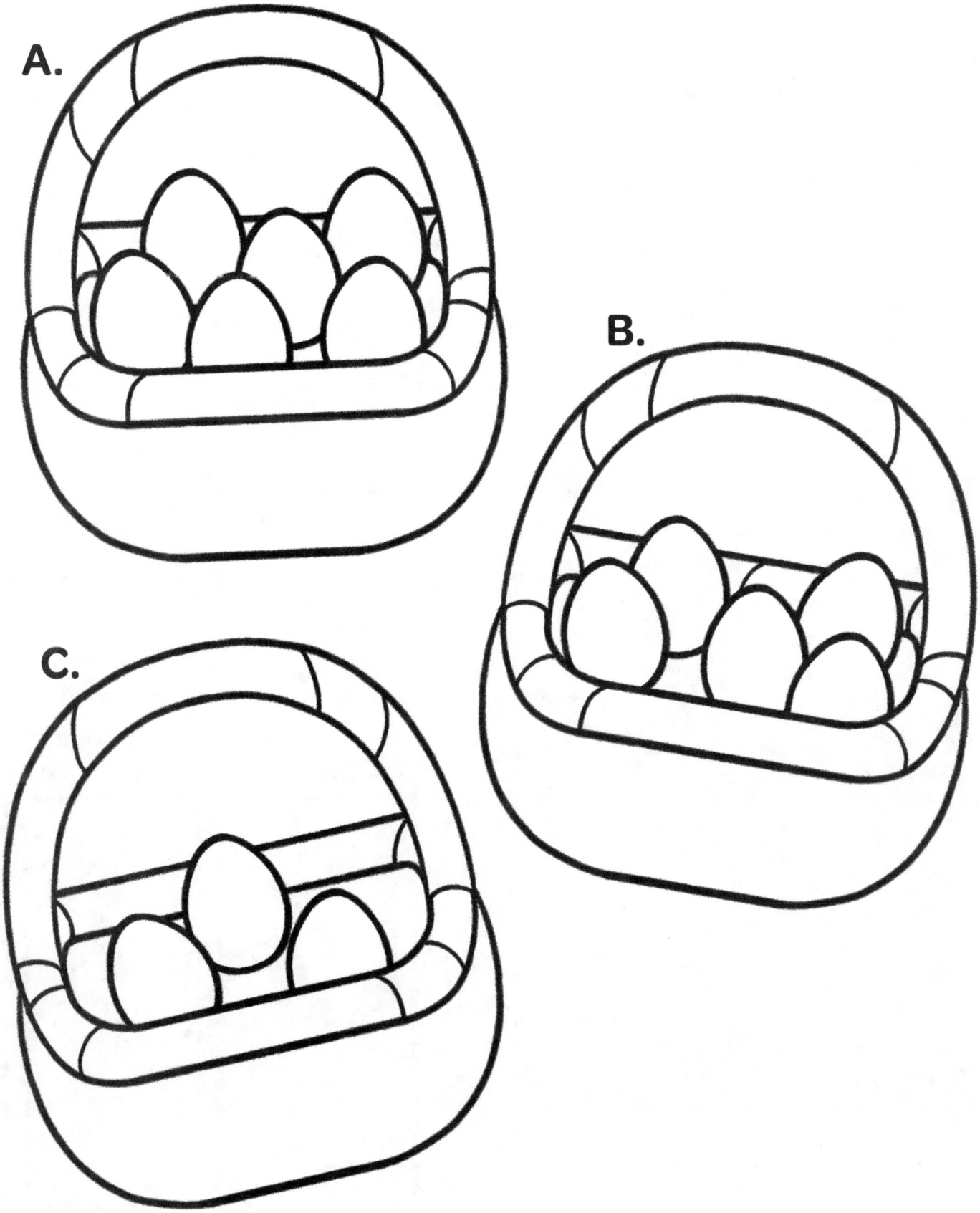


Answer: B

**Practice your shapes!**
**Draw some squares!**

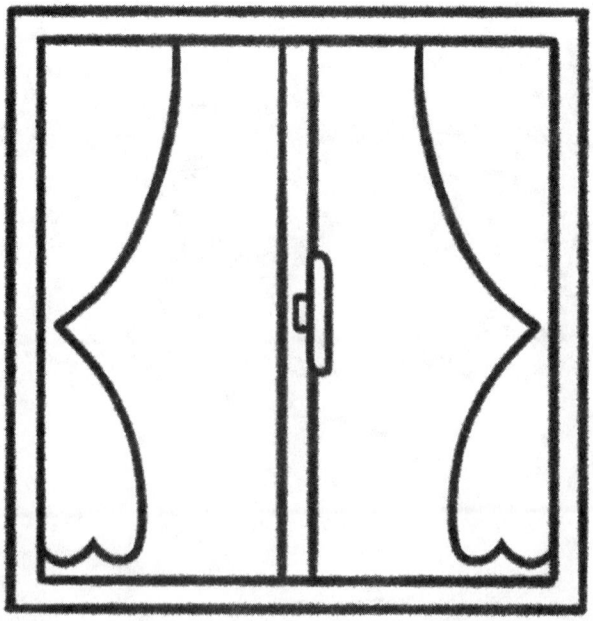

**Butterflies are beautiful!**
**Help this butterfly make its way to the flower.**

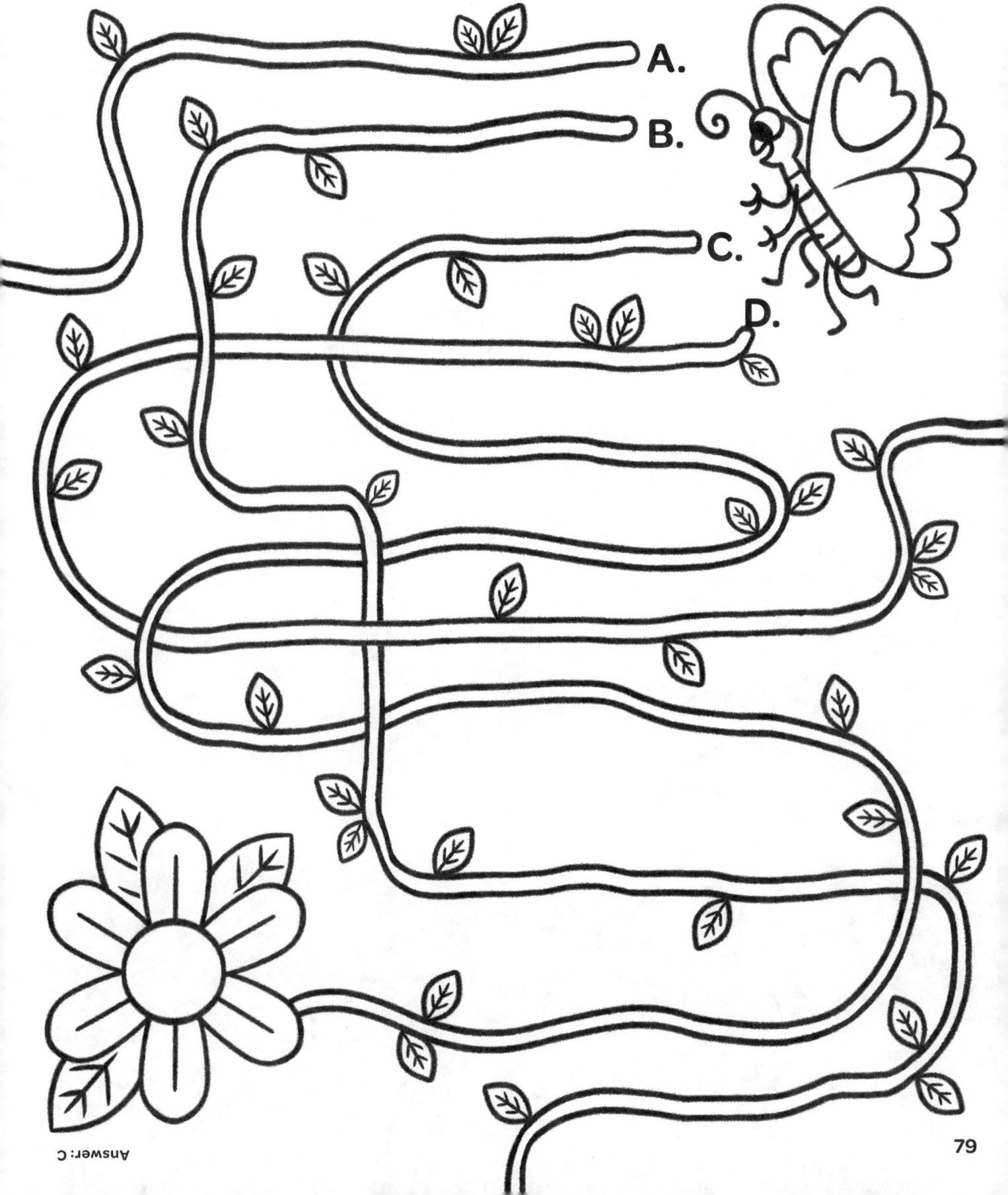


Answer: C

**This creature lives in its shell!**
**Connect the dots to reveal what it is.**

Spot the three differences in this scene!

Answers on page 191

Match the objects that go together!

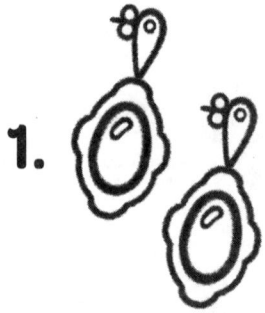


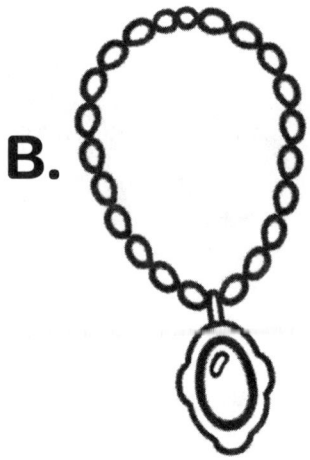


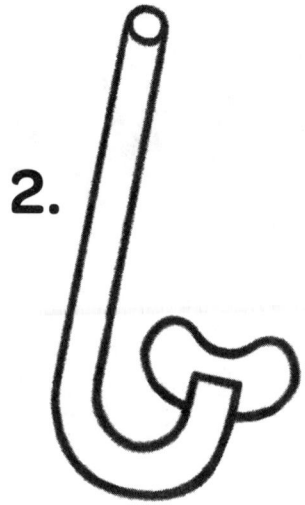

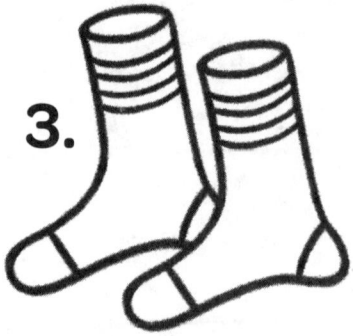




Answer: A-3, B-1, C-2

***Neigh!*** **Draw this unicorn's fantastical horn!**

Put these events in the correct order!

Answer: A-3, B-2, C-1

**Do you like to wear dresses?**
**Design your dream dress!**

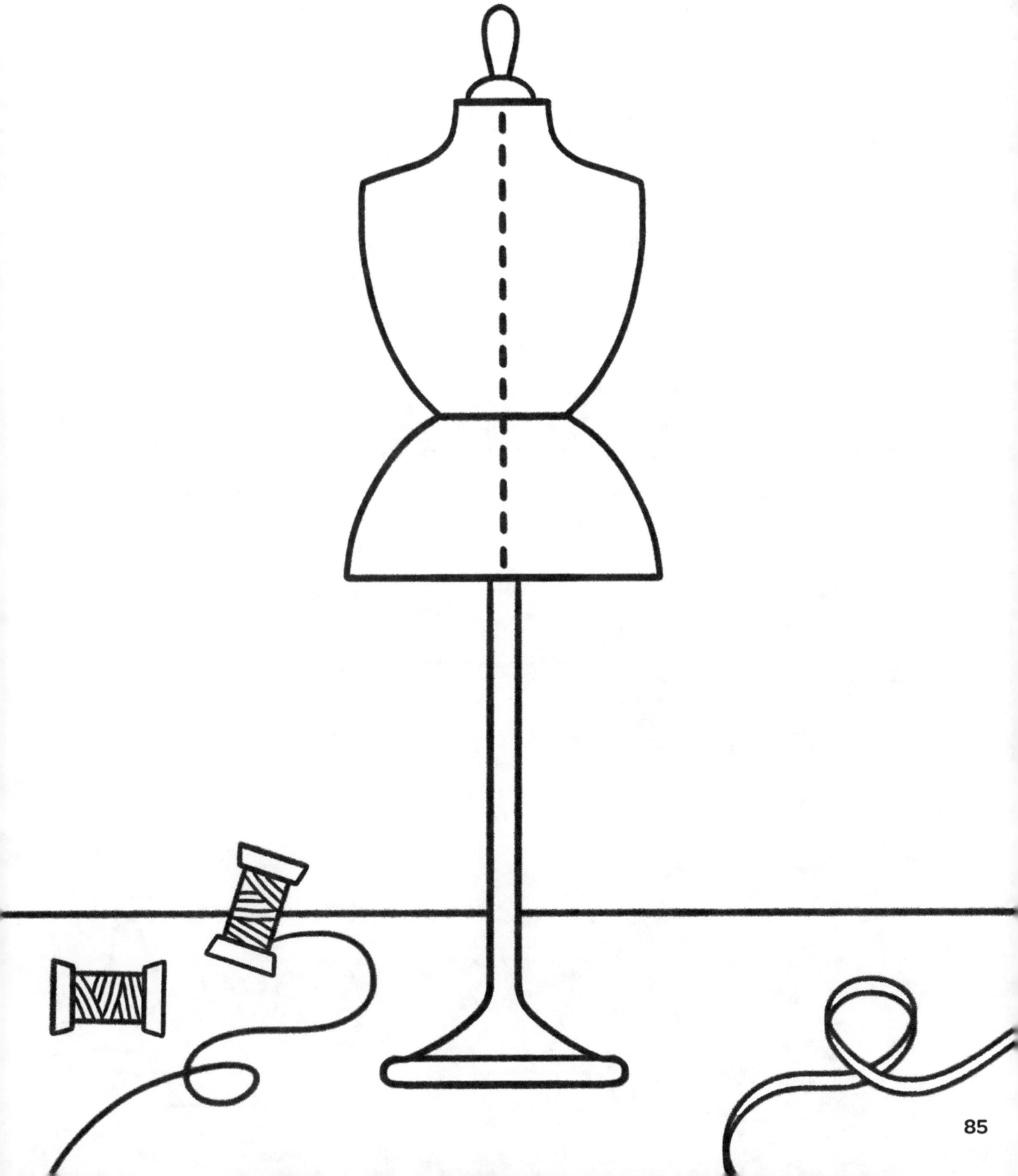

***Woof! Woof!*** **Help the puppy get to his bone!**

Answers on page 191

**Practice your shapes!**
**Draw some rectangles!**

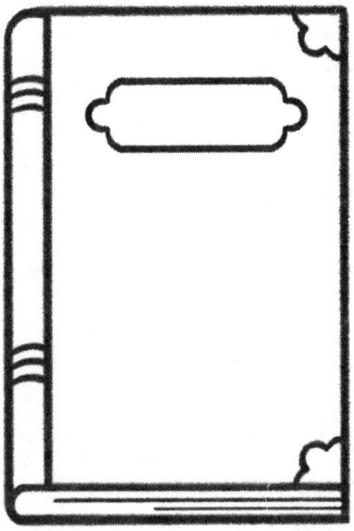

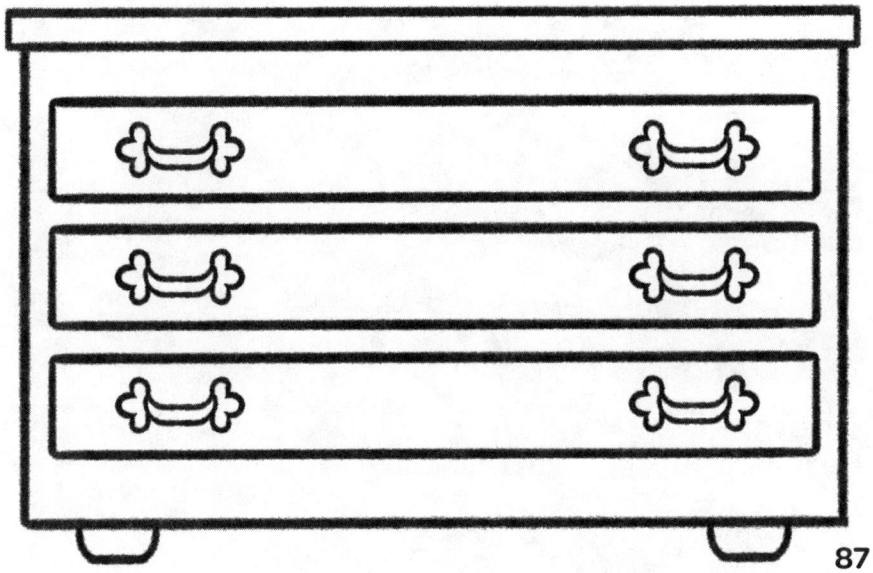

Draw some dotted lines to create rain coming from the cloud!

***Oink! Oink!*** **Can you get this little piggy back to the mud puddle?**

Answers on page 191

**Connect the dots to reveal a bird that you'll see at ponds or lakes!**

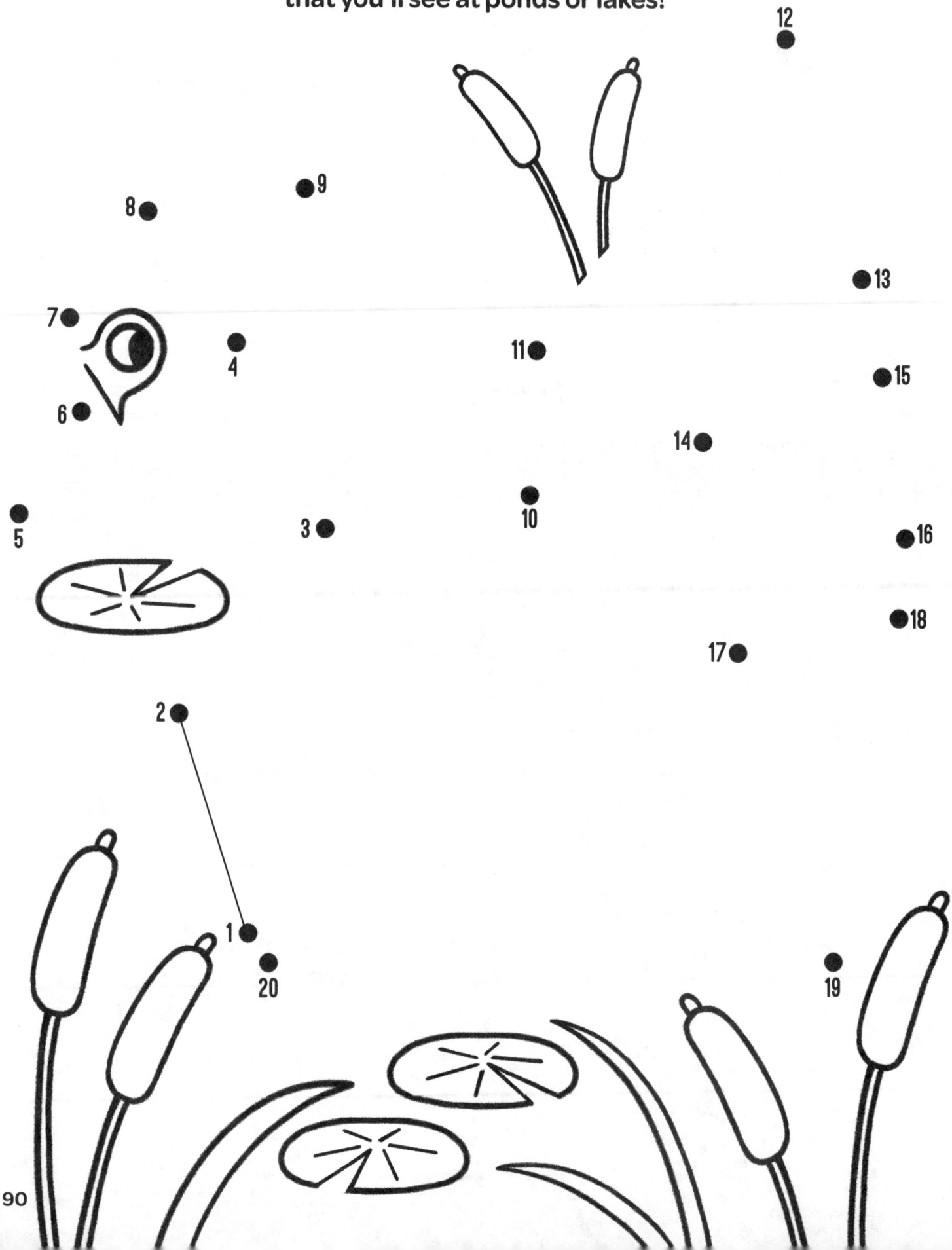

Spot the three differences in this scene!

Answers on page 191

**Match the shoes to make three pairs!**

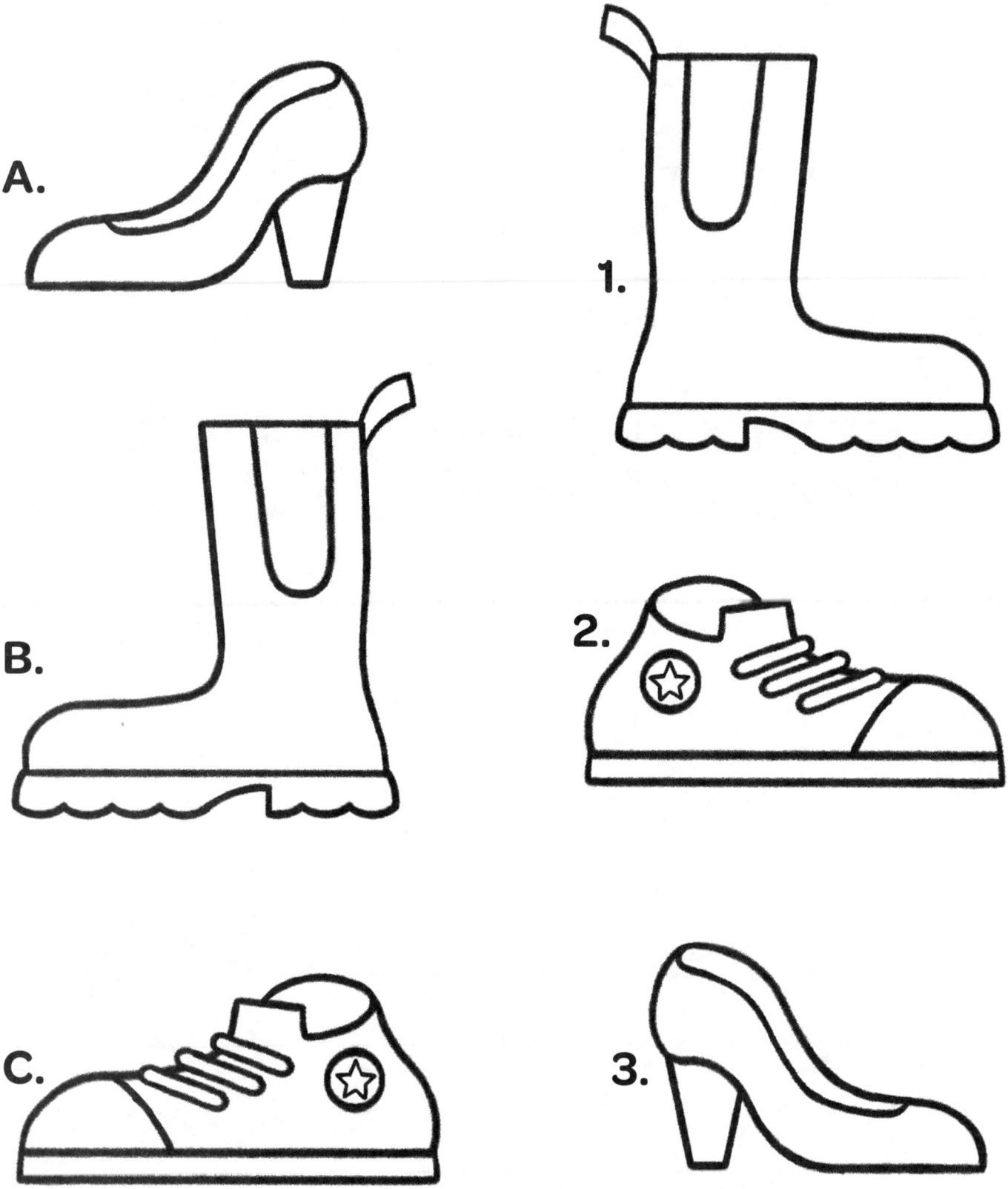


Answer: A-3, B-1, C-2

**Draw a crown fit for a queen!**

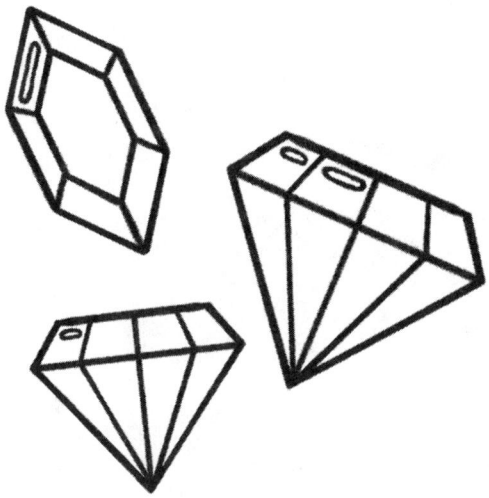

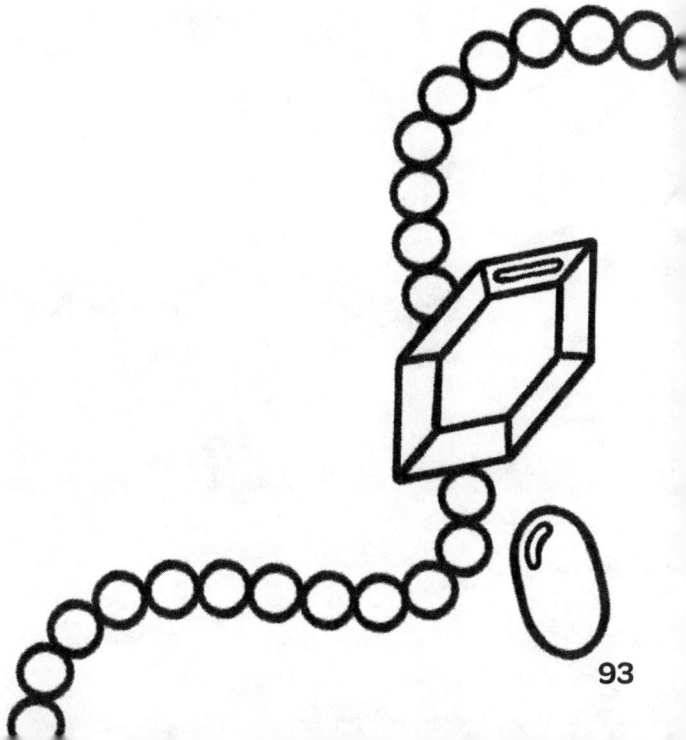

A baby koala is called a joey!

**Trains are a lot of fun!**
**Color in the train below.**

***Zzzz!*** **This sloth looks sleepy.**

**Draw zigzagging lines to create lightning bolts coming from the cloud!**

## Finish the patterns!

Answers on page 191

**You've finished your snack!**
**Can you help get the banana peel to the compost bin?**

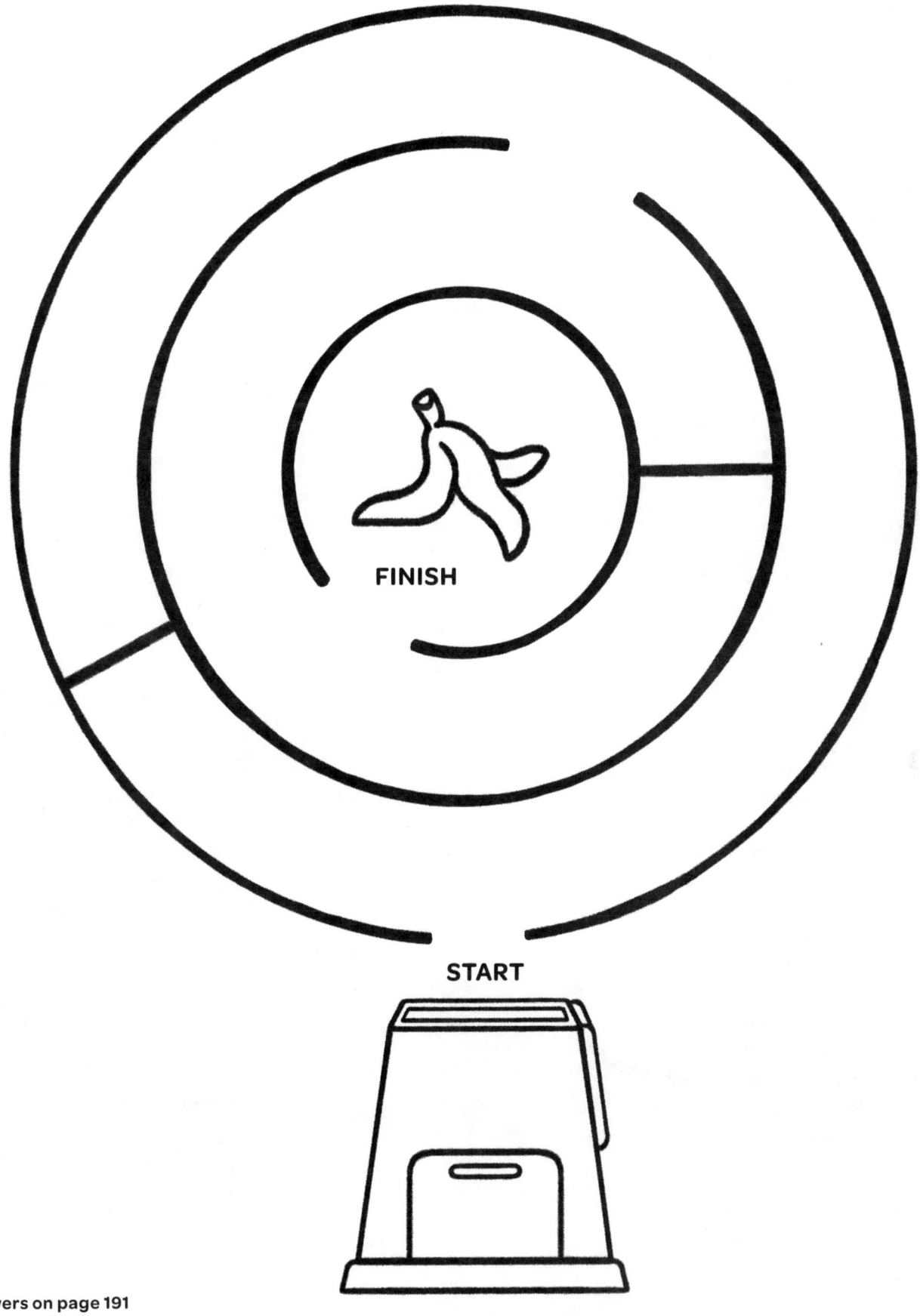


Answers on page 191

Connect the dots to complete this rainbow!

Spot the three differences in this scene!

Answers on page 191

## Can you find the matching butterflies?

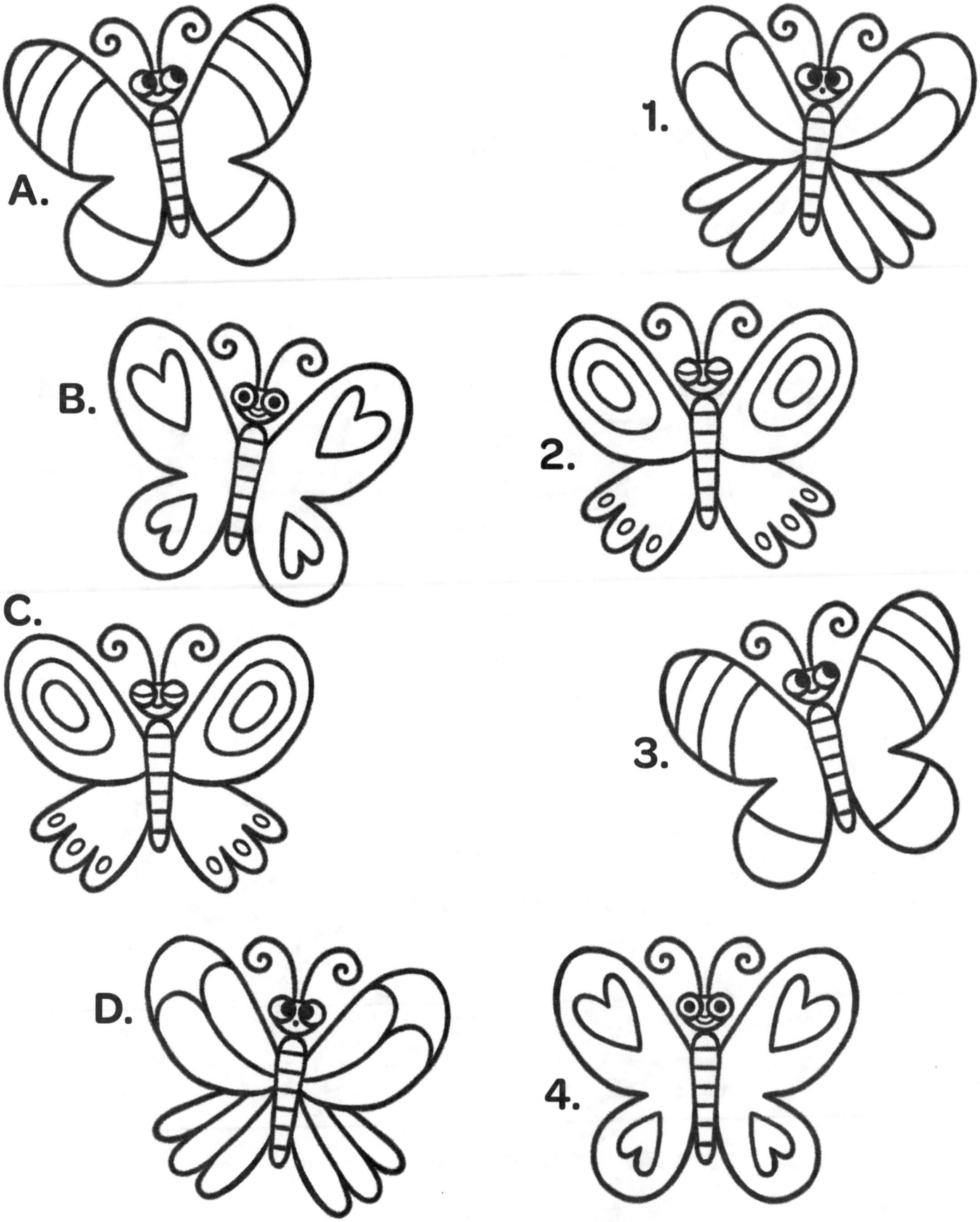


Answer: A-3, B-4, C-2, D-1

***Boom! Boom!*** **Draw some fireworks to light up the sky.**

Gorillas are one of the biggest and most powerful primates alive!

**It's a perfect day to go to the beach!**
**Decorate the sandcastle.**

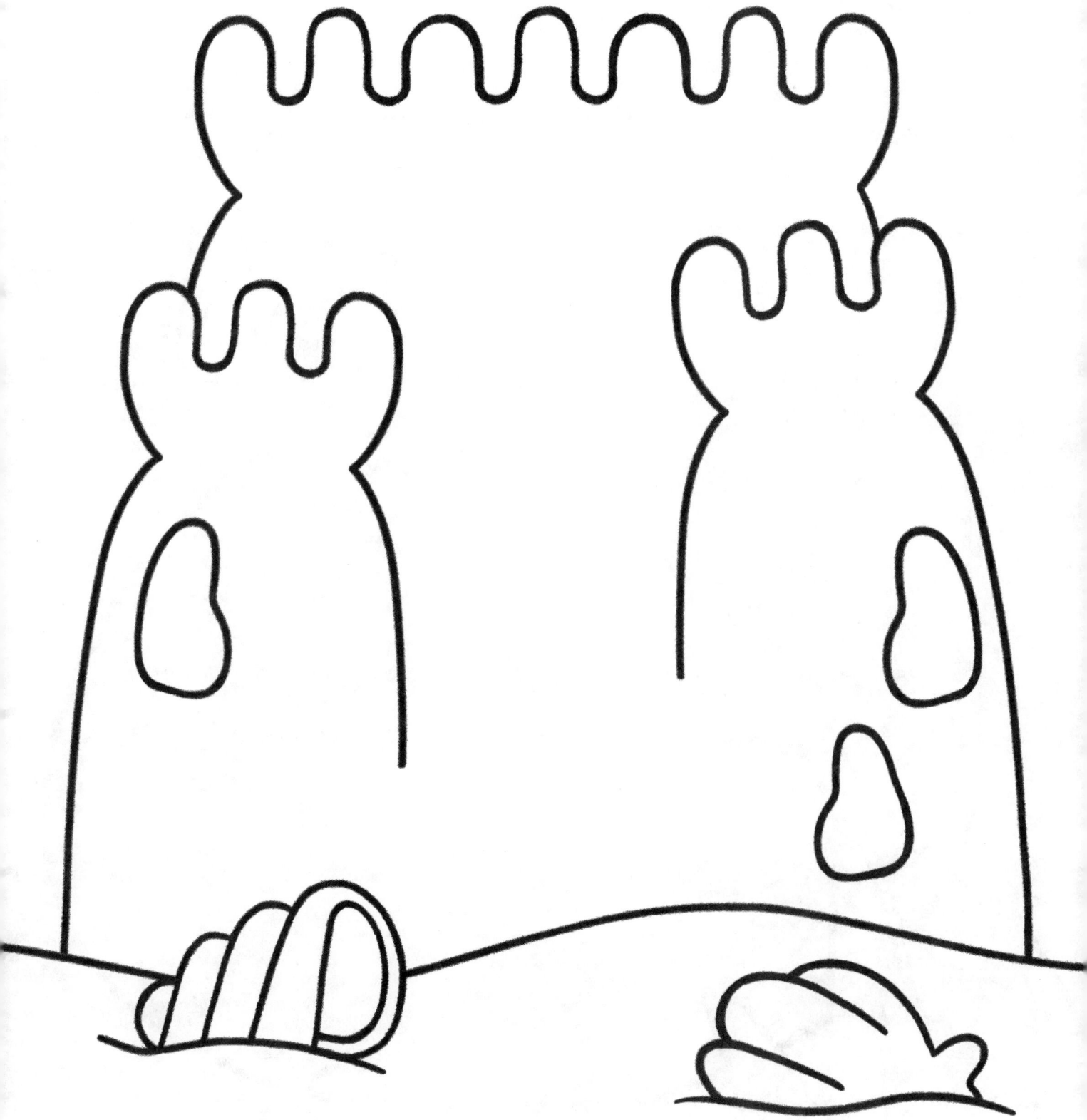

The pond is empty!
Can you add two lily pads?

**Practice your shapes!**
**Draw some diamonds!**

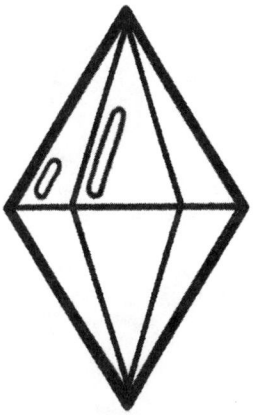

**Draw your perfect tree house!**

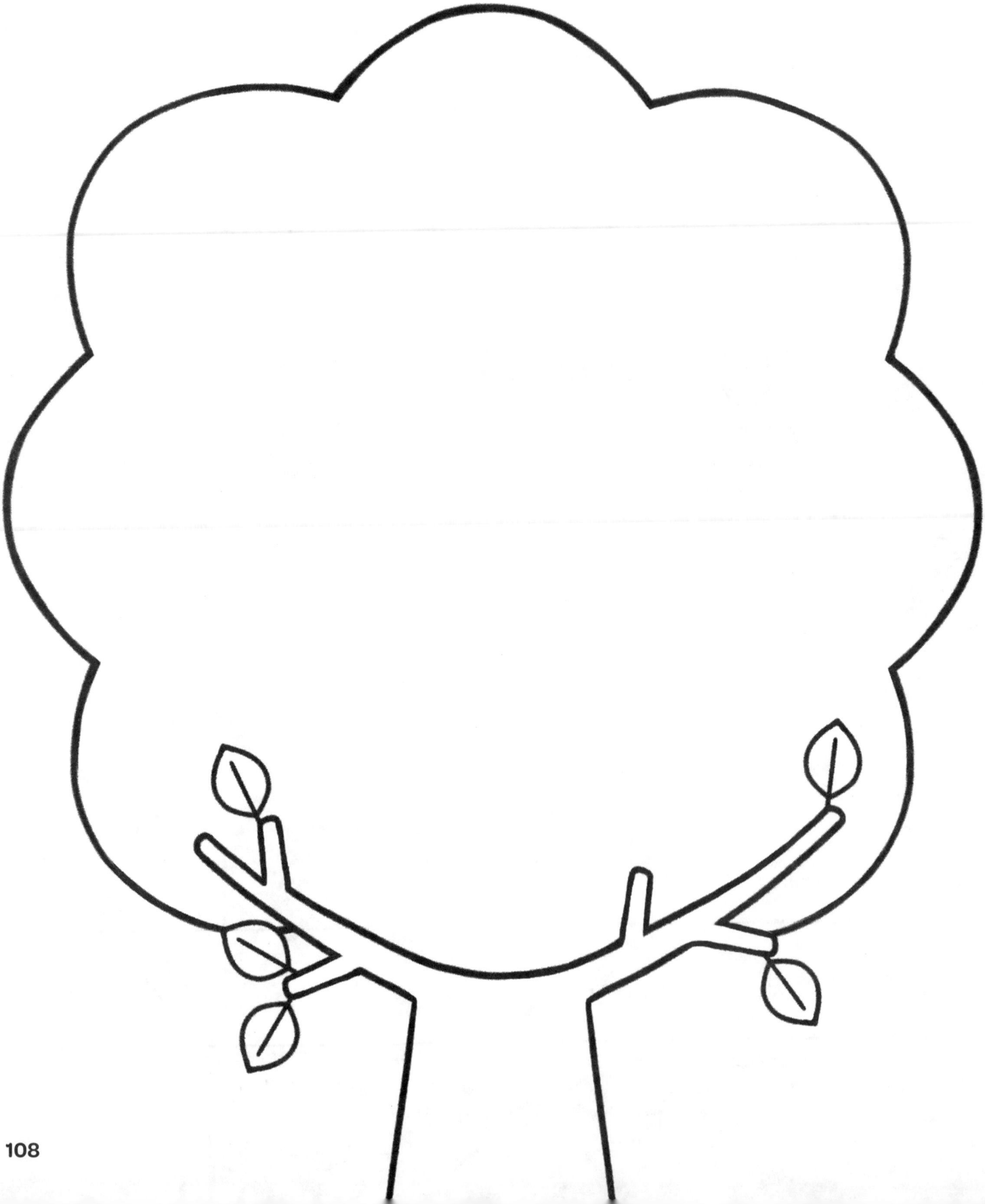

**Mice love cheese! Can you help this mouse get to the block of cheese?**

Answers on page 191

**Connect the dots to reveal a delicious dessert!**

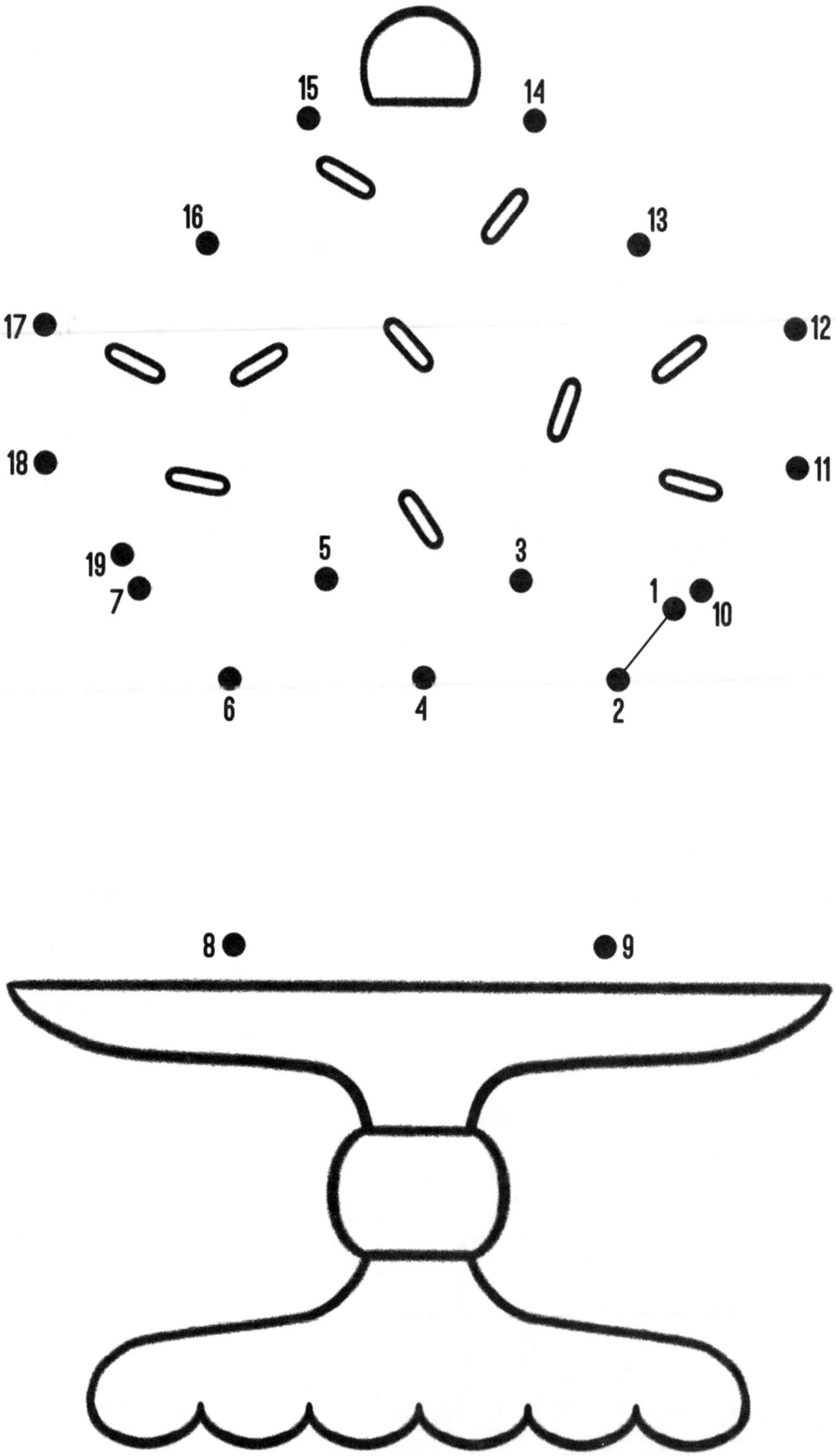

**Spot the three differences in this scene!**

Answers on page 191

**Did you know tress give off oxygen?**
**Match the trees below!**

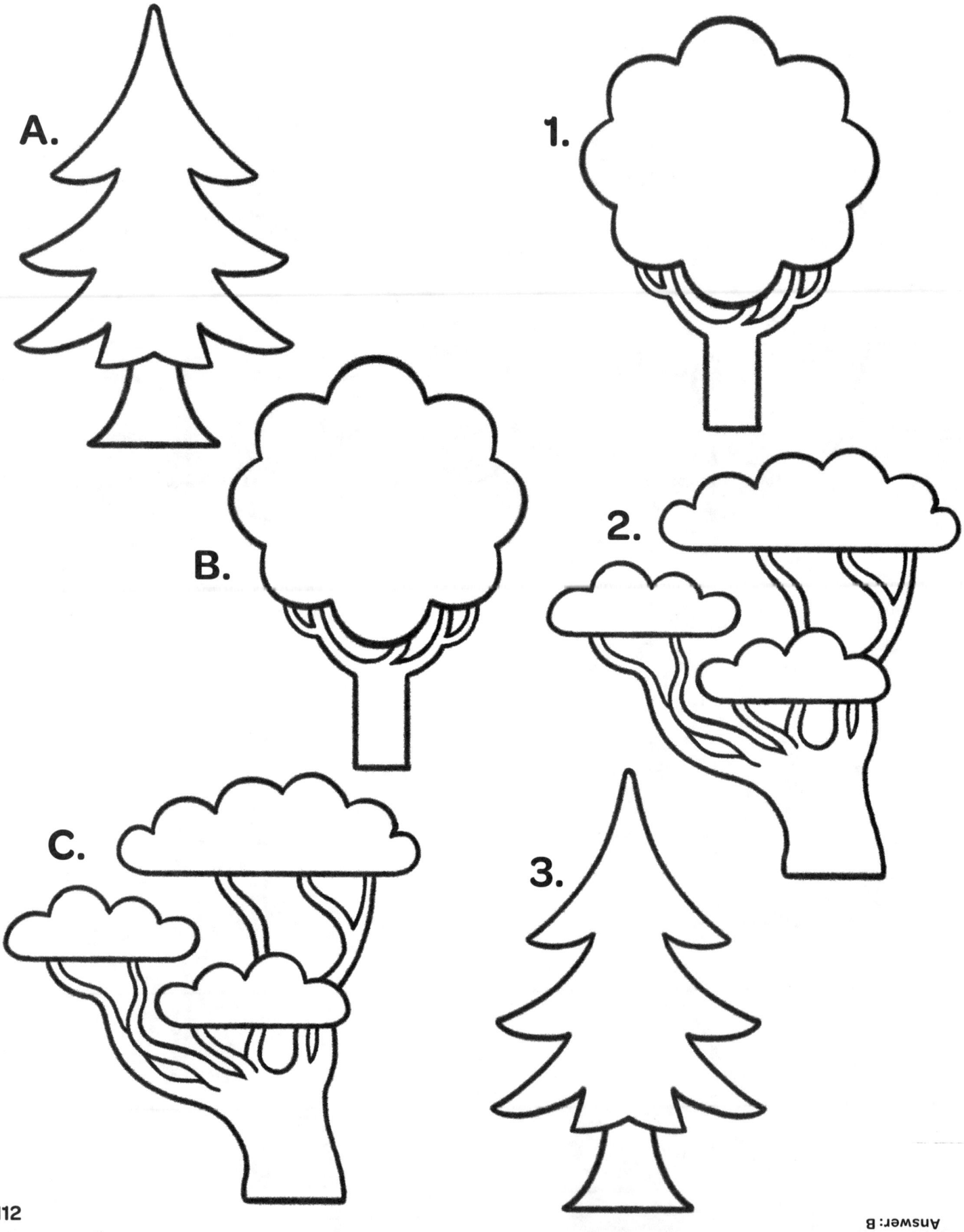




Answer: B

***Beep! Boop!*** **Create your own robot. What would you name it?**

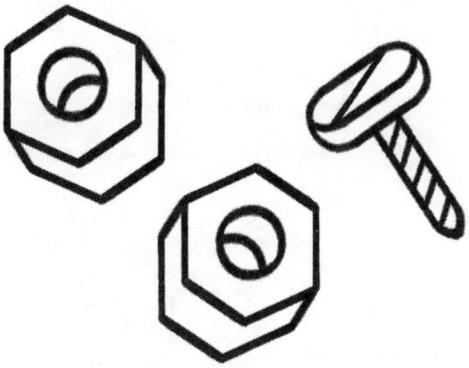

Did you know there were over 700 species of dinosaurs?

**Decorate this birdhouse to put in the garden!**

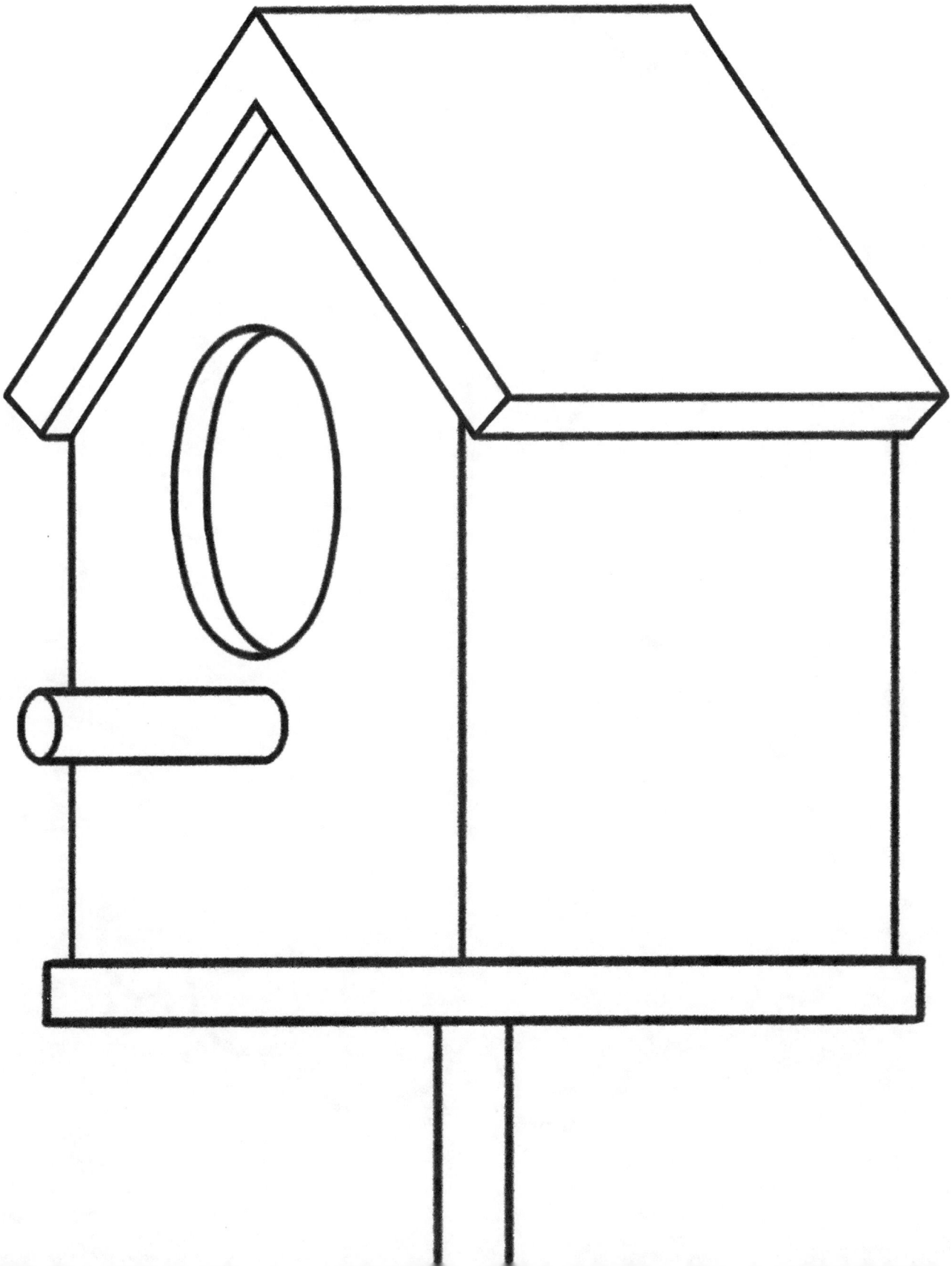

Clams live in the ocean!
Add one pearl to the center of the clam.

## Finish the patterns!

Answers on page 191

Match the food to its flavor!

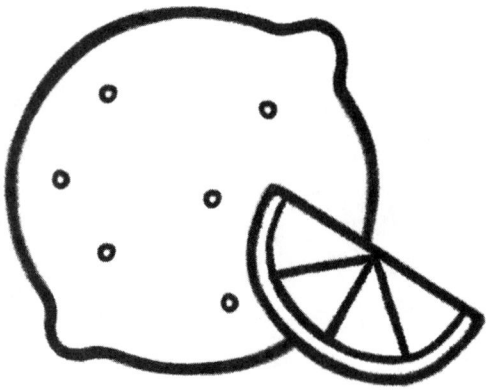

SAVORY

SOUR

SPICY

SWEET



Answers on page 191

**Whales are huge! Can you help this whale find his way back to the ocean?**

Answer: A

**These fish have plenty of sharp teeth, but they are picky eaters!**
**Connect the dots to see what it is!**

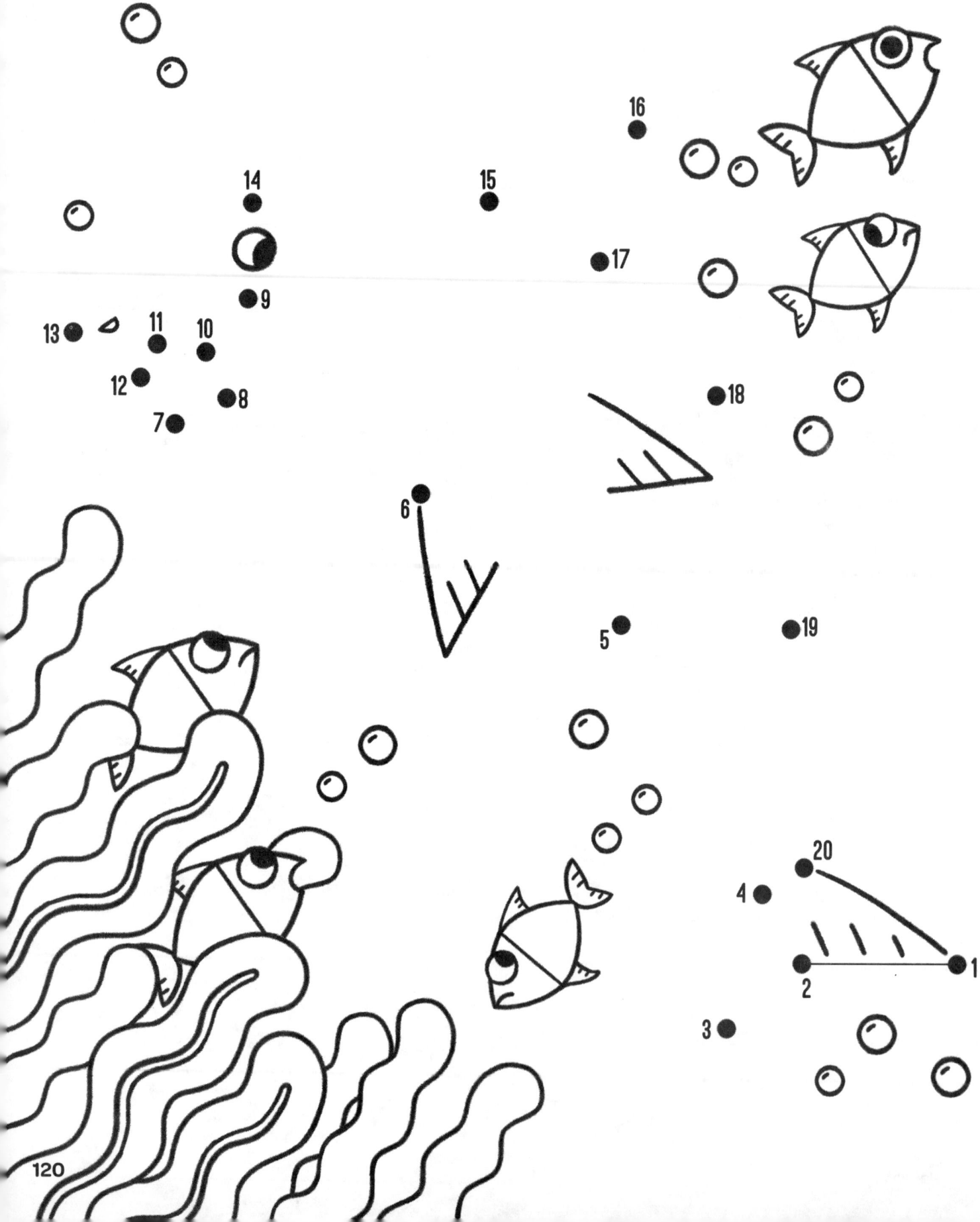

Spot the three differences in this scene!

Answers on page 191

**Can you match each animal to its favorite food?**

Answer: A-3, B-1, C-2

**Fill the treasure chest below with your greatest treasures!**

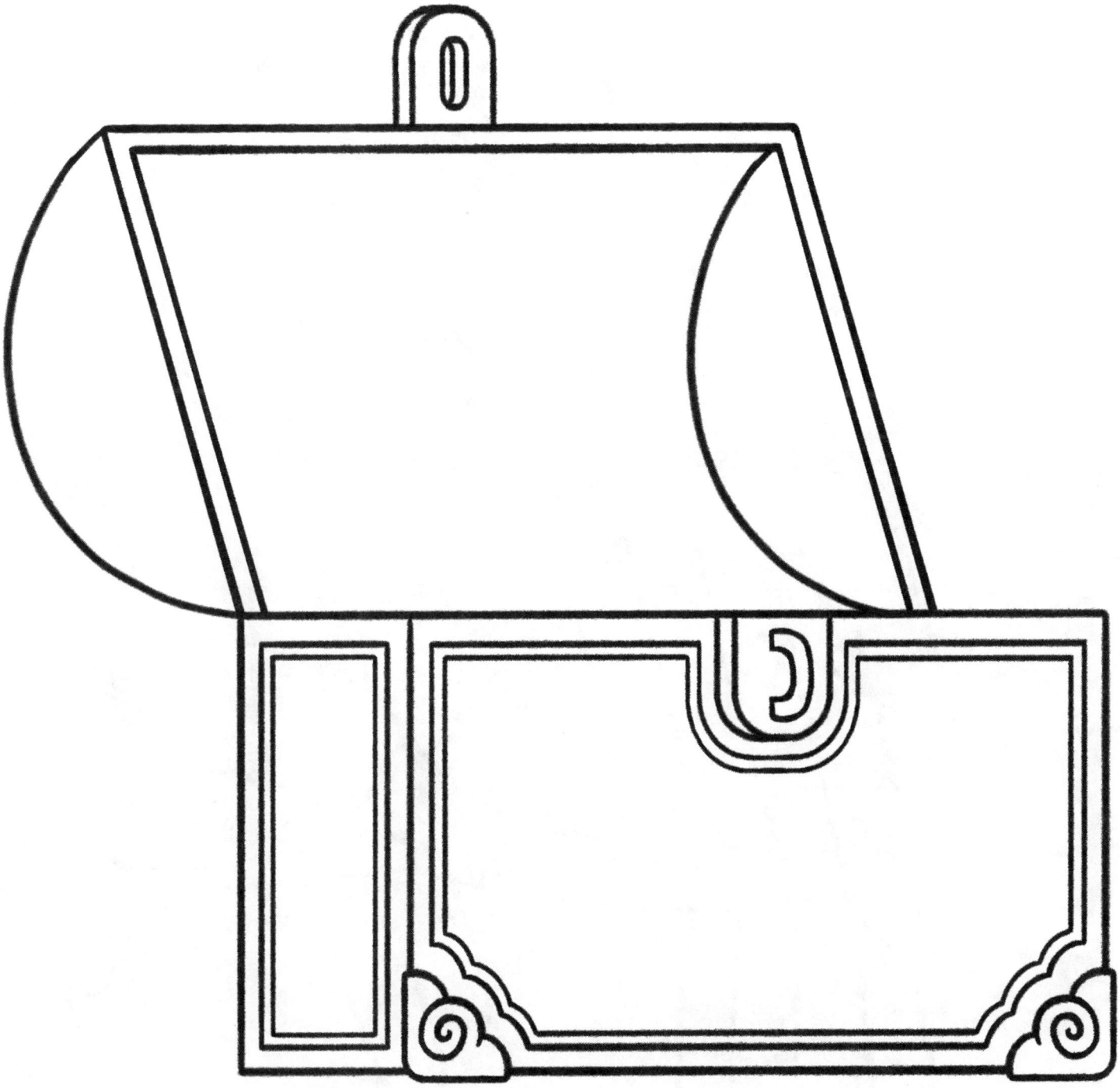

Parrots are thought to be one of the smartest birds!

Color in this beautiful rainbow!

**Giraffes are tall!**
**Add three spots to the giraffe below.**

Circle the person wearing glasses!

Answer: C

**Put these events in the correct order!**

Answer: A-3, B-2, C-1

**Don't forget to recyle!**
**Can you help get this plastic bottle to the recycling bin?**

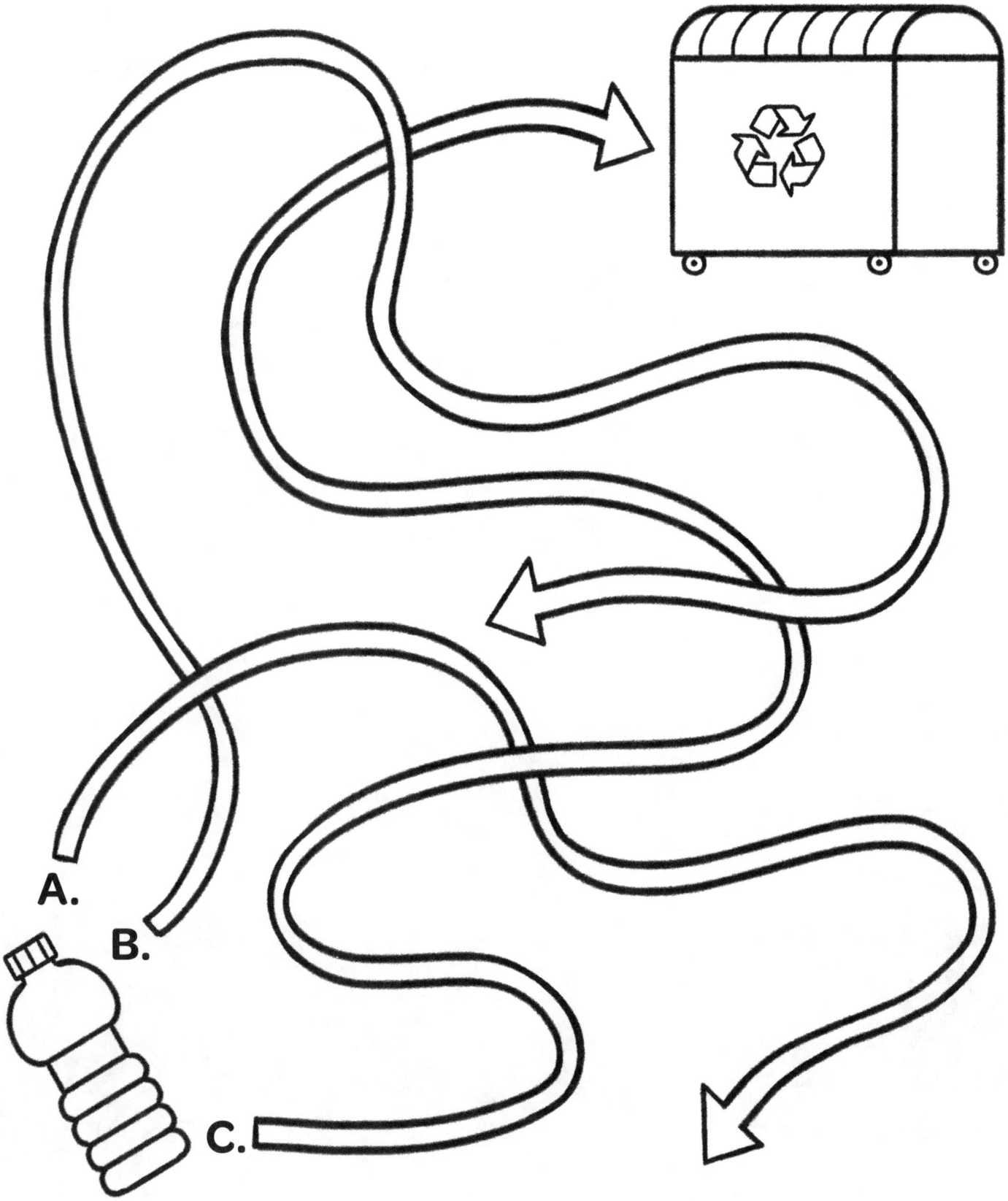


Answer: C

**These invertebrates are older than dinosaurs!**
**Connect the dots to reveal what it is!**

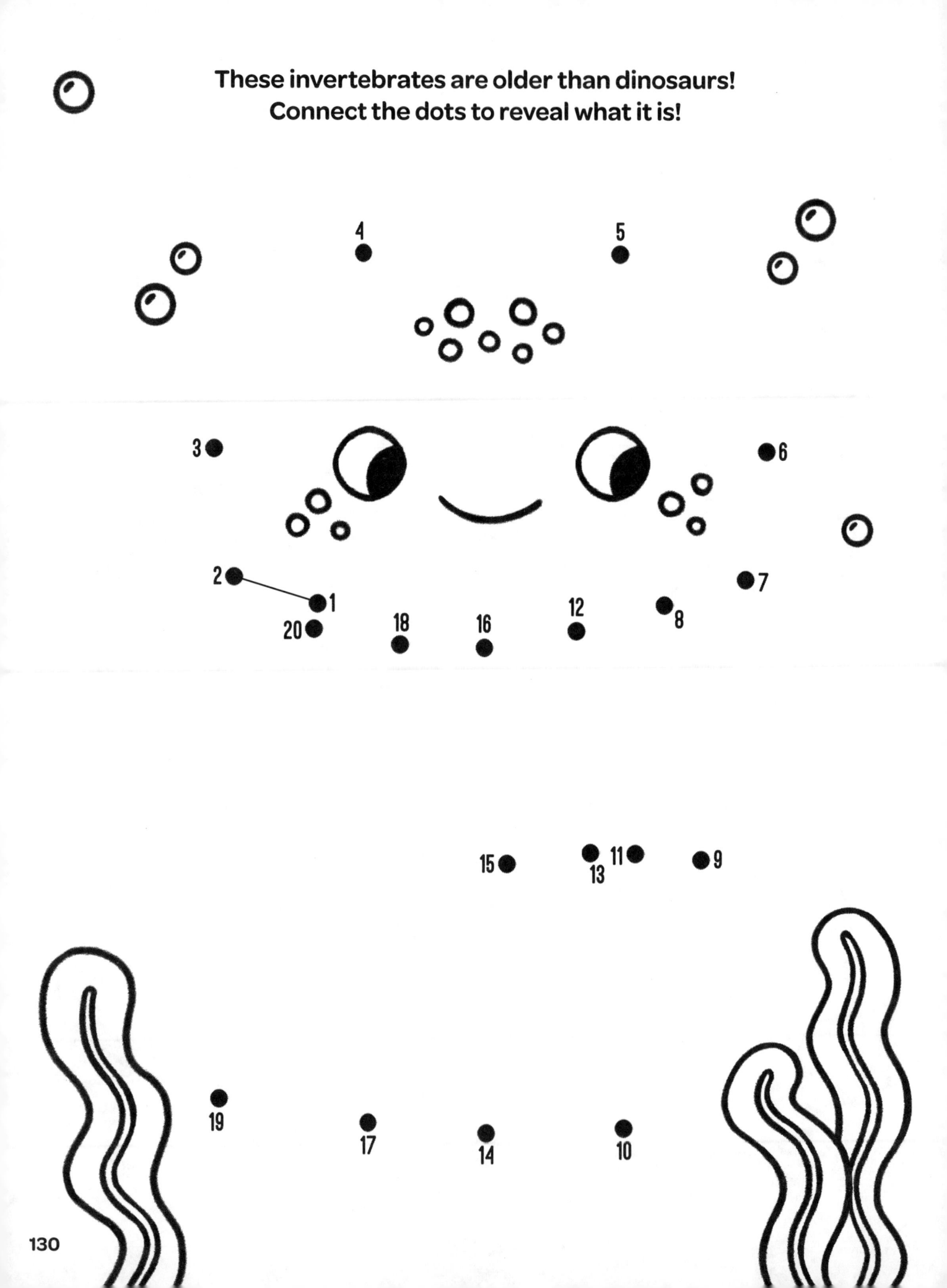

**Spot the three differences in this scene!**

Answers on page 191

**Let's play! Can you match the sports equipment that belongs together?**

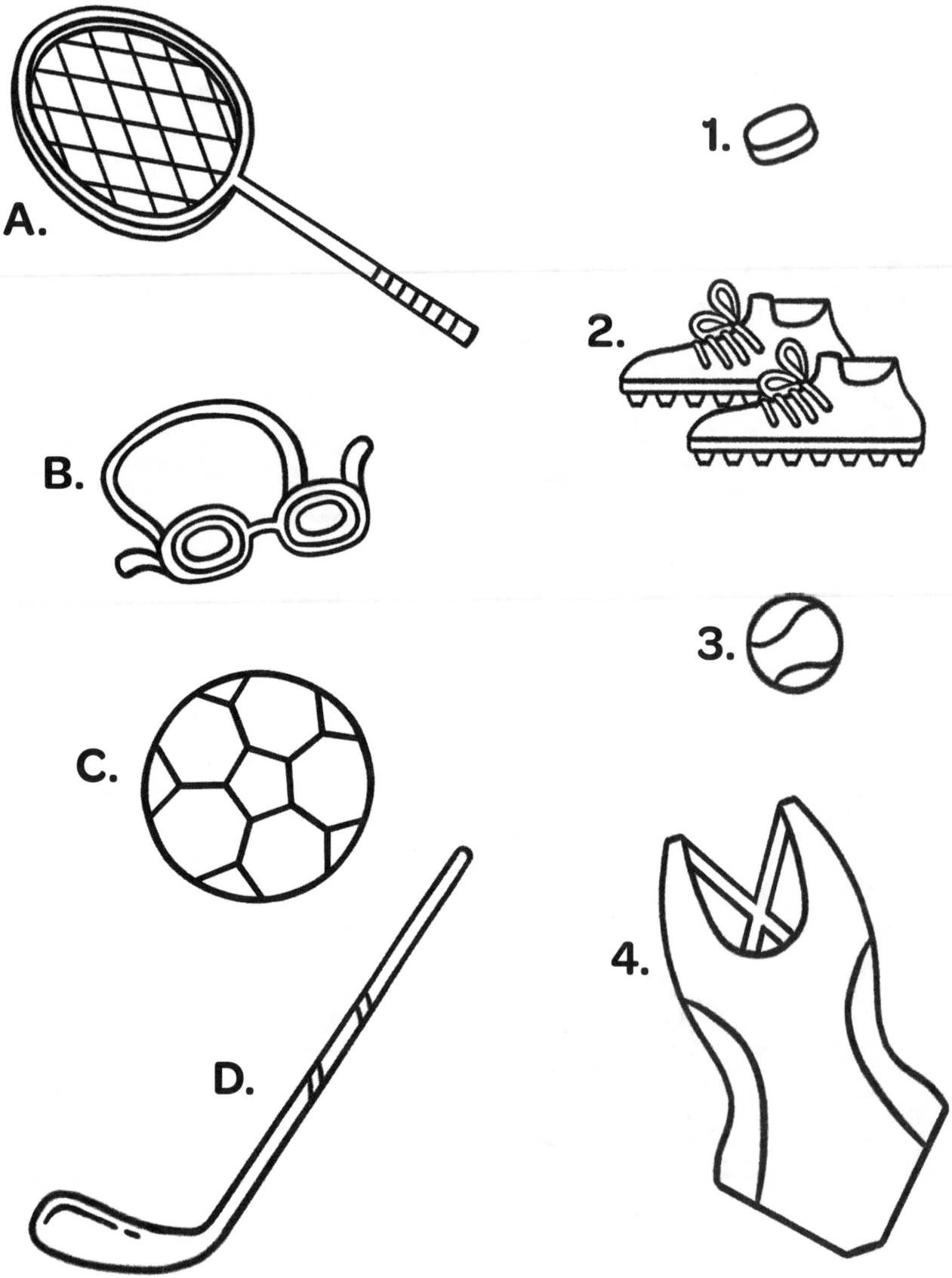


Answer: A-3, B-4, C-2, D-1

It's windy! Design a kite you'd love to fly.

**What would your rocket ship look like?**
**Color it in below!**

Decorate this cupcake any way you'd like!

**What a beautiful sunset!**
**Add two birds flying in the sky!**

Dragons are awesome mythical creatures!

Color each crayon with the color on its label!

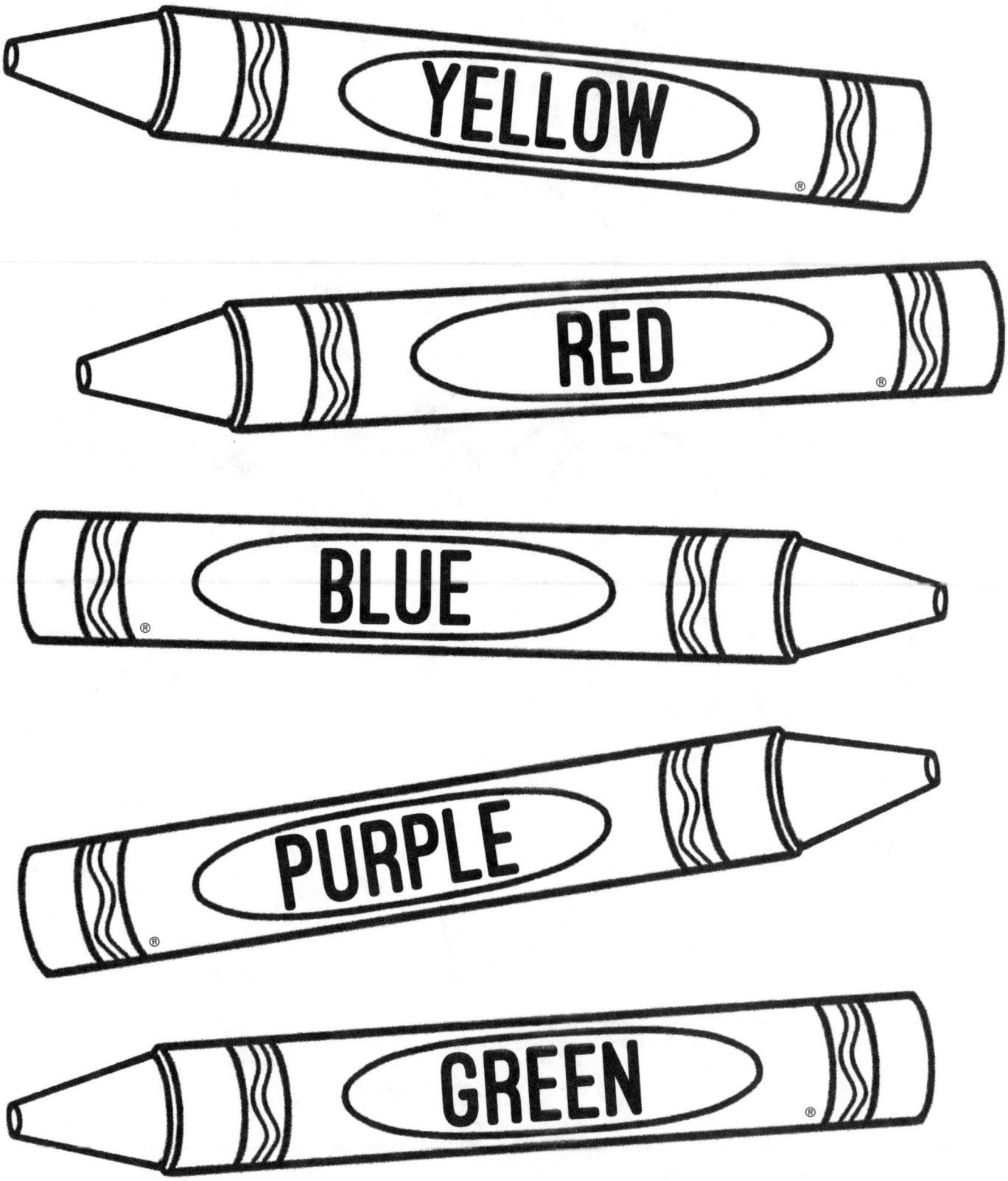

**Pirates love treasure!**
**Help the pirate find the treasure chest!**

Answers on page 191

Connect the dots to reveal a dinosaur!

Spot the three differences in this scene!

Answers on page 191

**Match each animal to its outline!**

Answer: A-2, B-3, C-1

**Do you like plants and flowers?**
**Draw them growing in the garden.**

A caterpillar just hatched out of its egg!

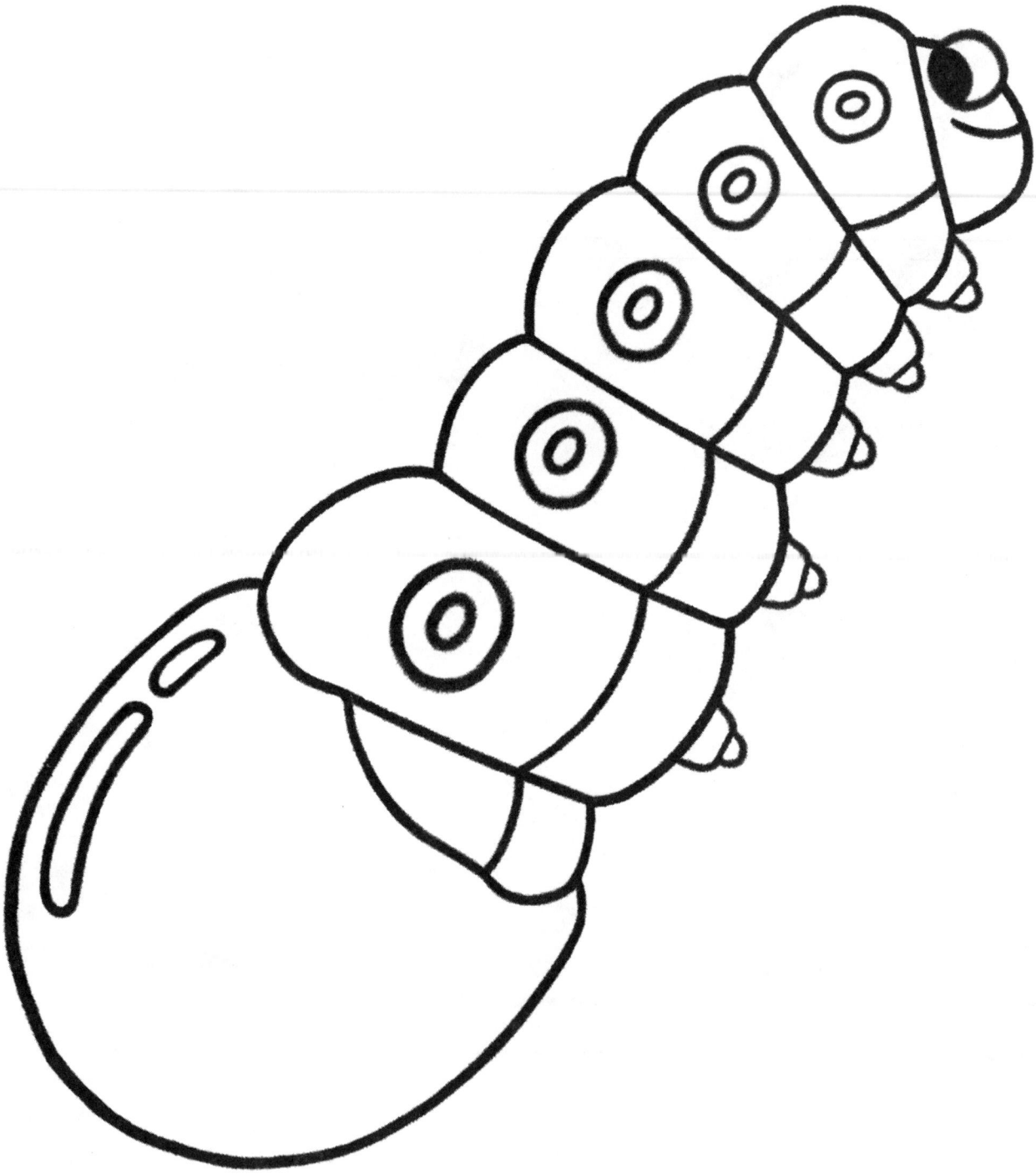

Anyone can be a knight in shining armor!

**This field looks a little empty!**
**Can you add three trees?**

## Finish the patterns!

Answers on page 191

Put these events in the correct order!

Answer: A-2, B-3, C-1

It's time for a snack!
Can you help this bunny get to his carrot?

Answers on page 191

**It's a rainy day.**
**Can you connect the dots**
**to make a rain cloud?**

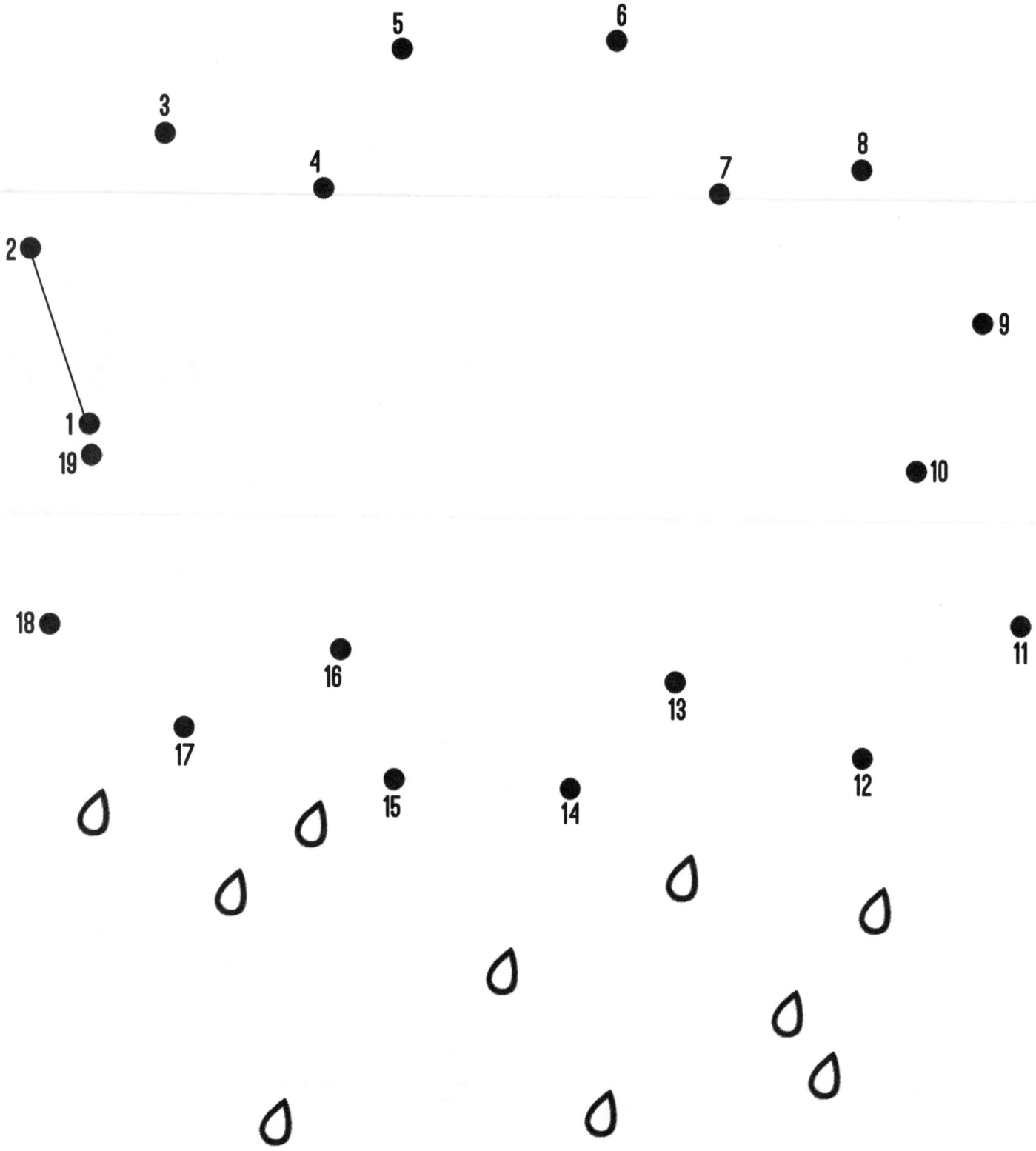

**Spot the three differences in this scene!**

Answers on page 191

Can you match each picture to its name?

LAMP

CAR

HOUSE

BALL



Answers on page 192

**What's your favorite animal?**
**Draw it below!**

**What's your favorite kind of donut?**
**Decorate the one below!**

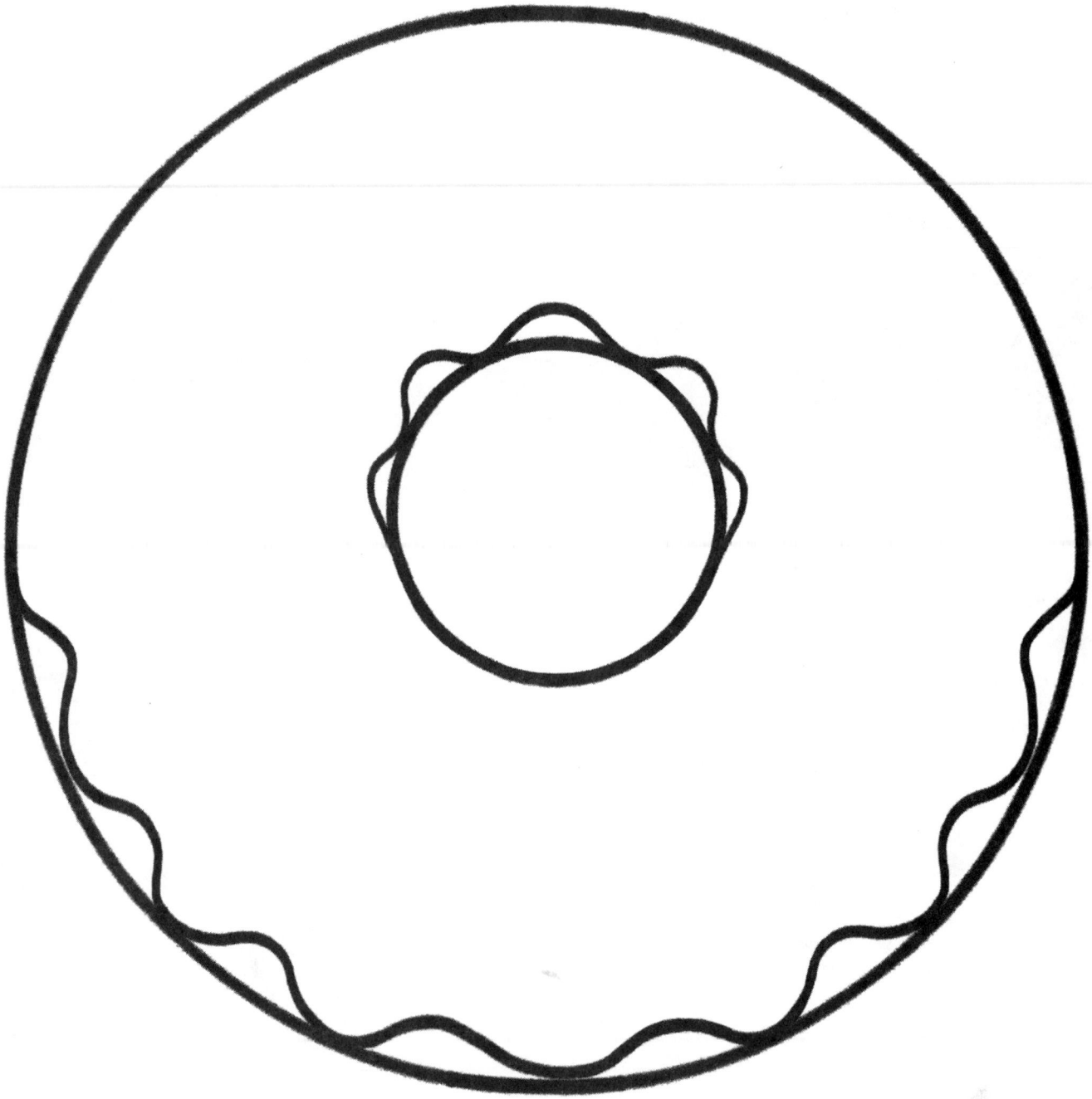

Decorate these cookies for a bake sale!

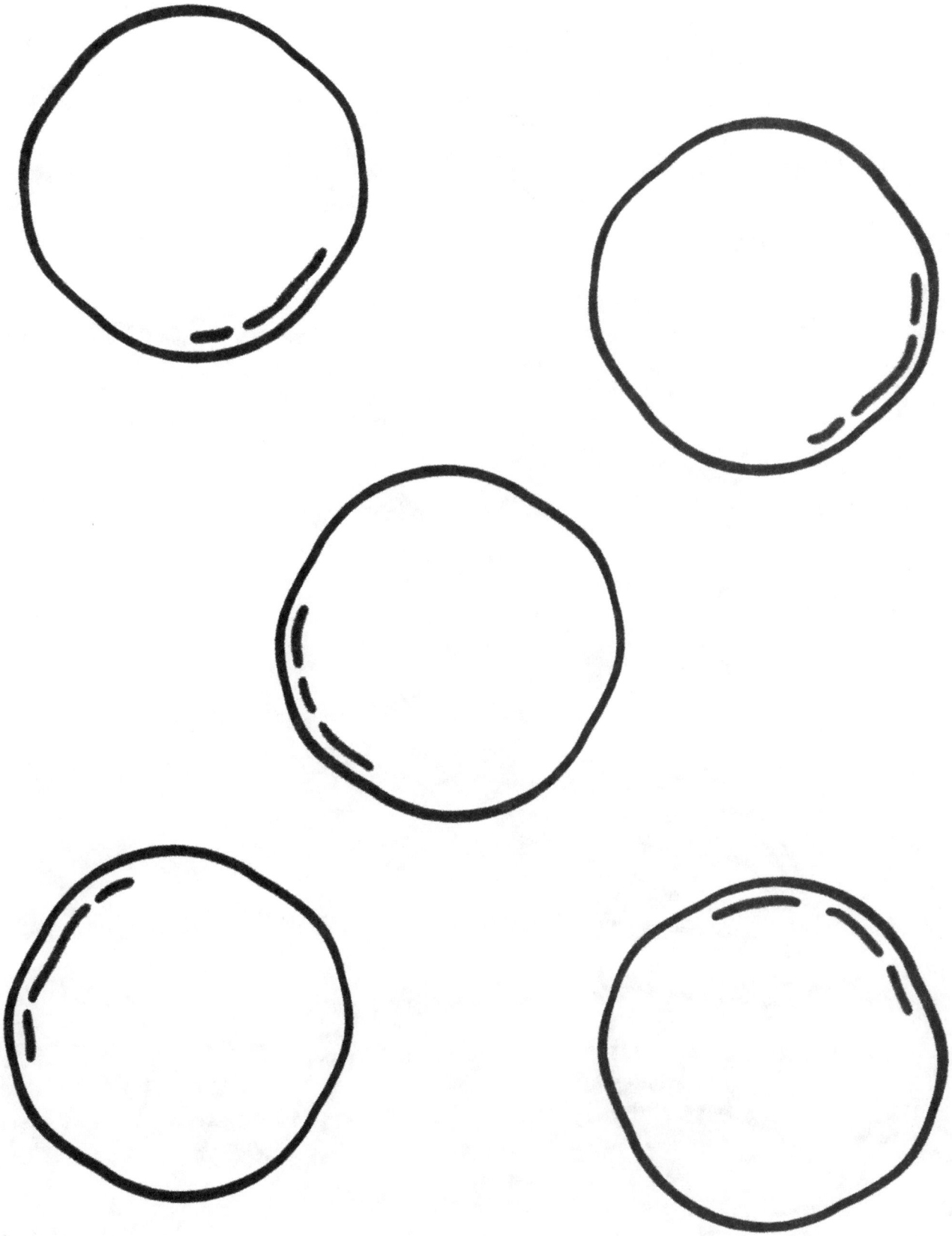

**The sand on the beach is nice and warm.**
**Add four seashells!**

Match each item to its shape!

SQUARE

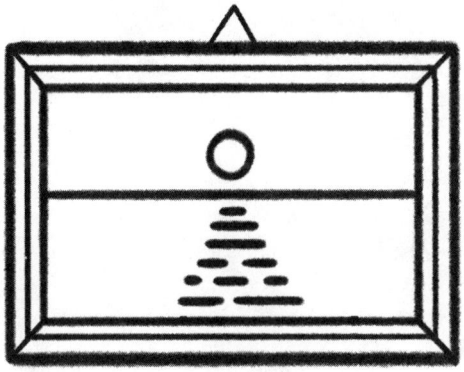

CIRCLE

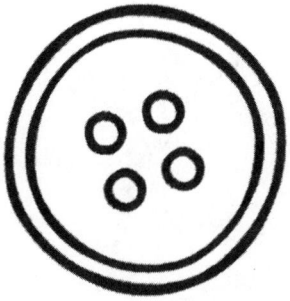

RECTANGLE

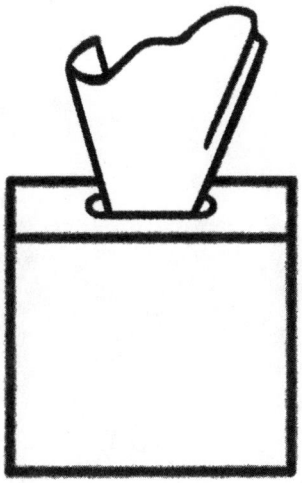

TRIANGLE

Answers on page 192

A group of zebras is called a dazzle.
Add some stripes to the zebra below!

***Buzz!*** **Can you help the bee get back to its hive?**

Answer: C

**Wow! Can you connect the dots to reveal what's flying through the sky?**

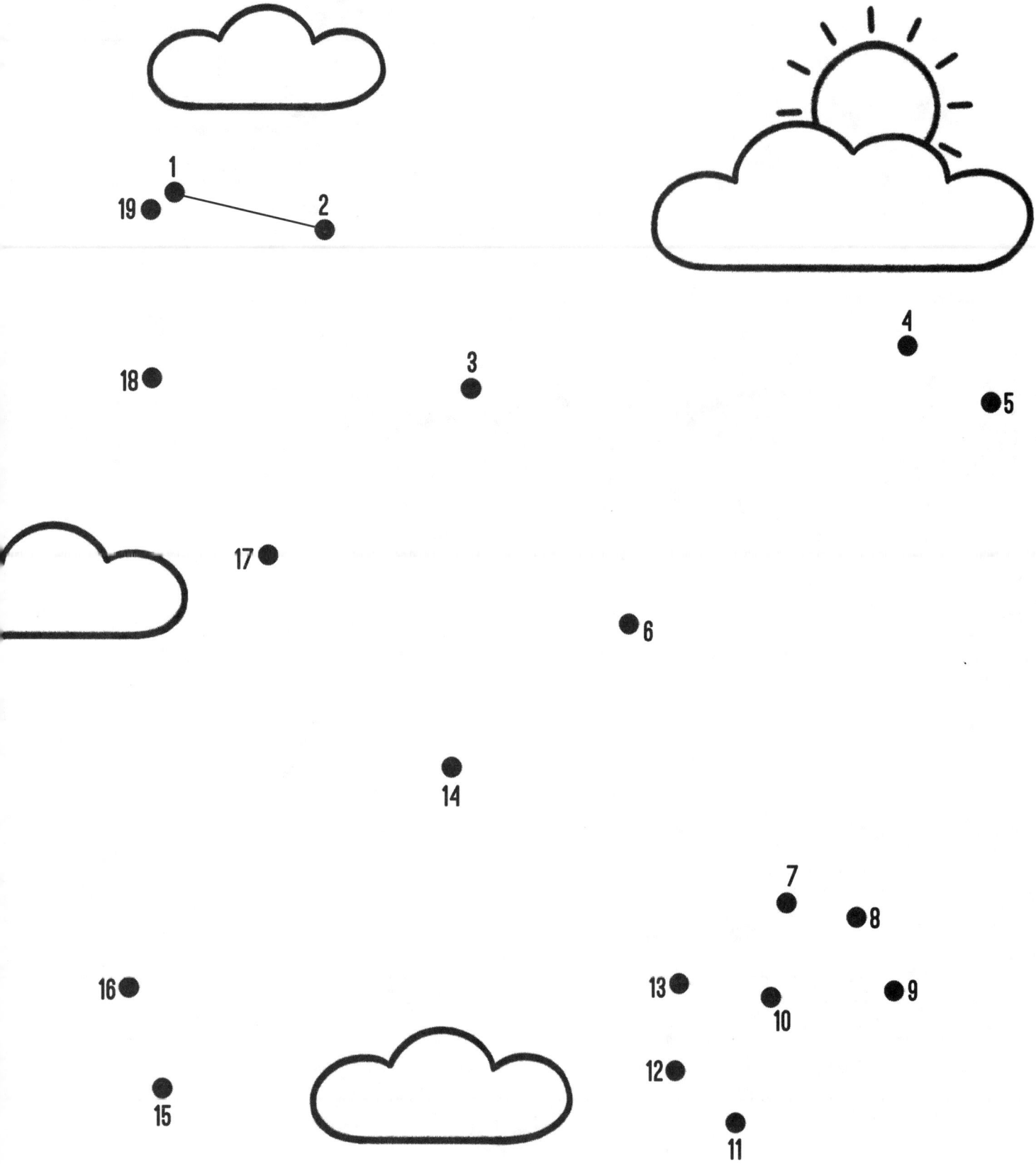

**Spot the three differences in this scene!**

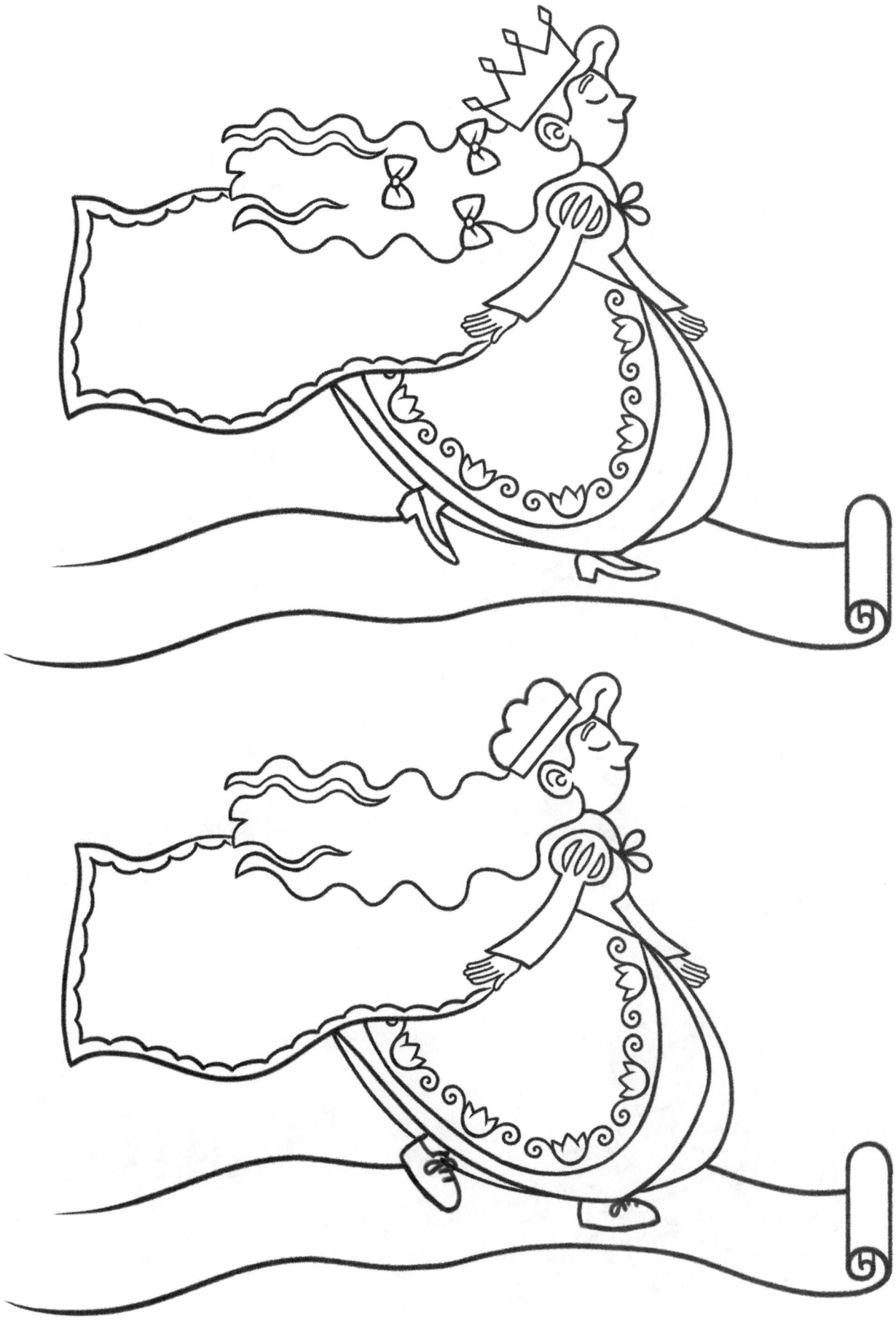

Answers on page 192

**Match each article of clothing to the appropriate season!**

FALL

SUMMER

SPRING

WINTER



Answers on page 192

It's a party! Draw some fun balloons!

This hot-air balloon flies high in the sky!

**Do you like sports?**
**Decorate your team's jersey!**

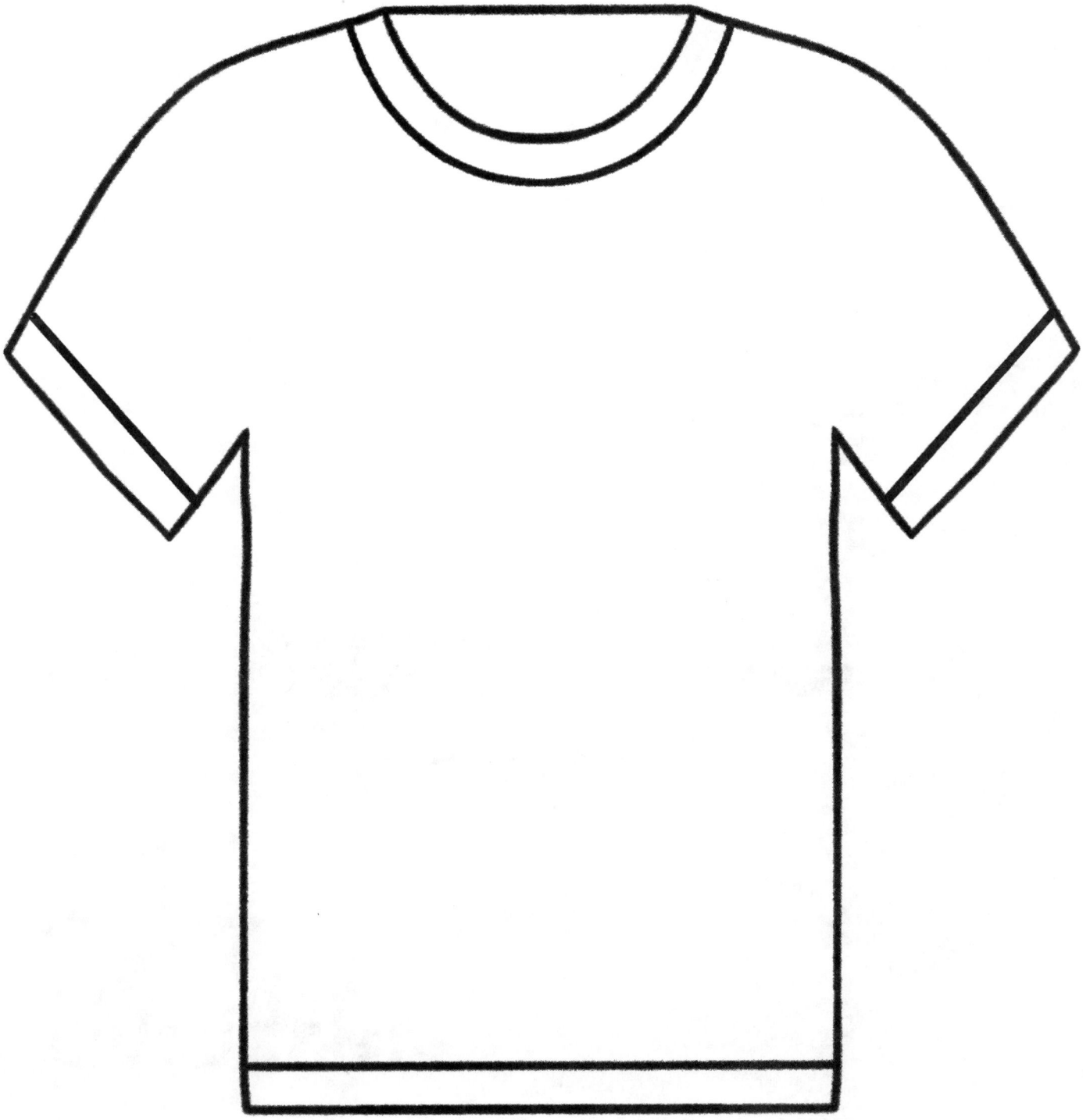

Match each item to its shape!

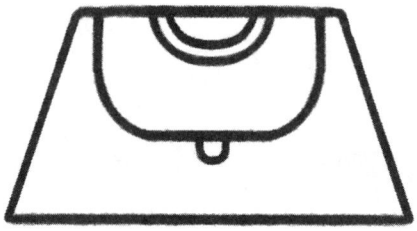

OVAL

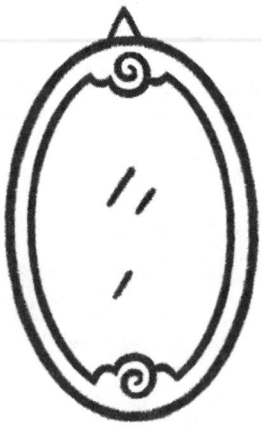

DIAMOND

STAR

TRAPEZOID



Answers on page 192

**Can you help the dragon fly back to the castle?**

Answers on page 192

**That sure is a big piece of construction equipment!**
**Connect the dots to reveal what it is.**

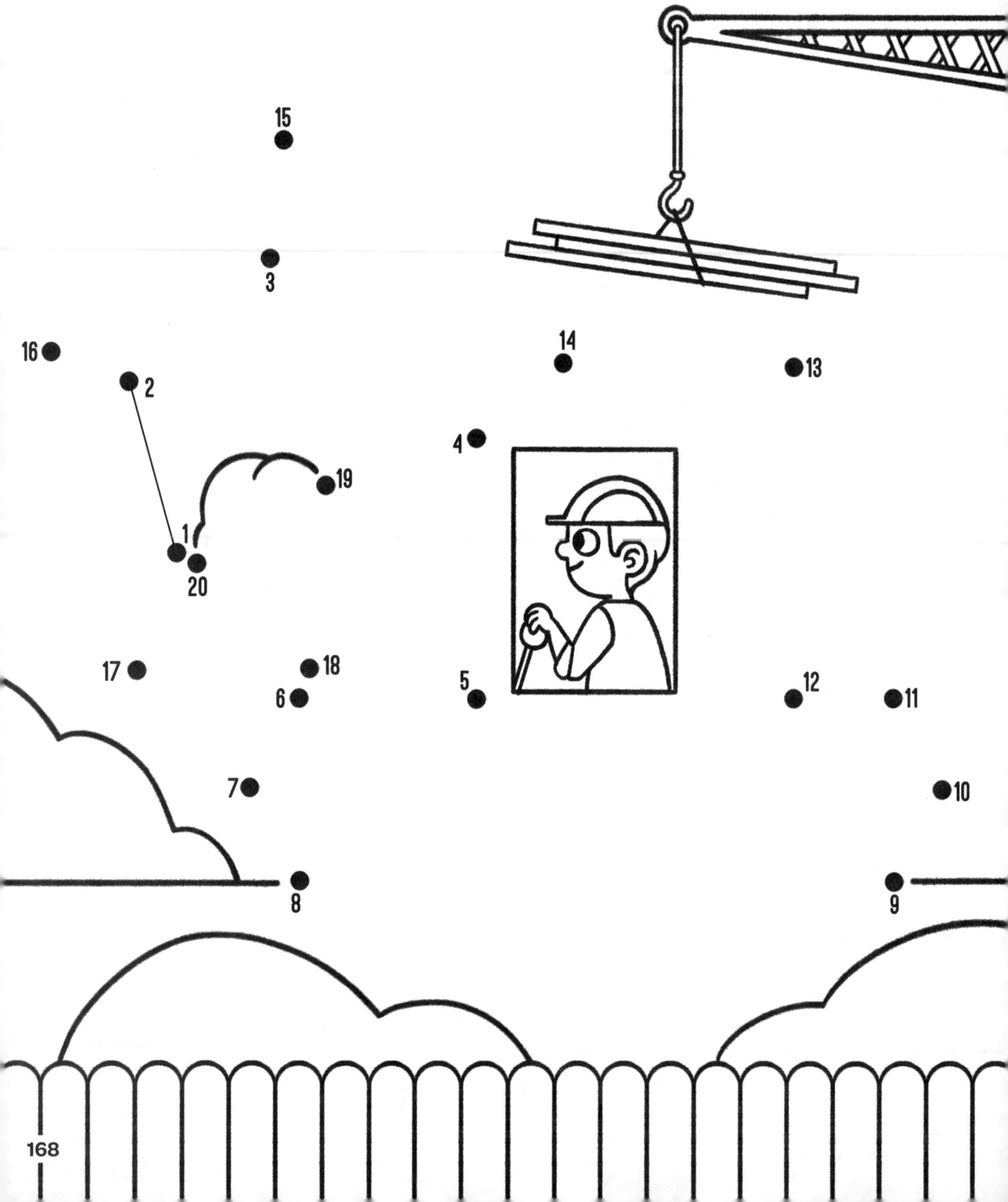

**Spot the three differences in this scene!**

Answers on page 192

**Bundle up! Can you match up these mittens?**

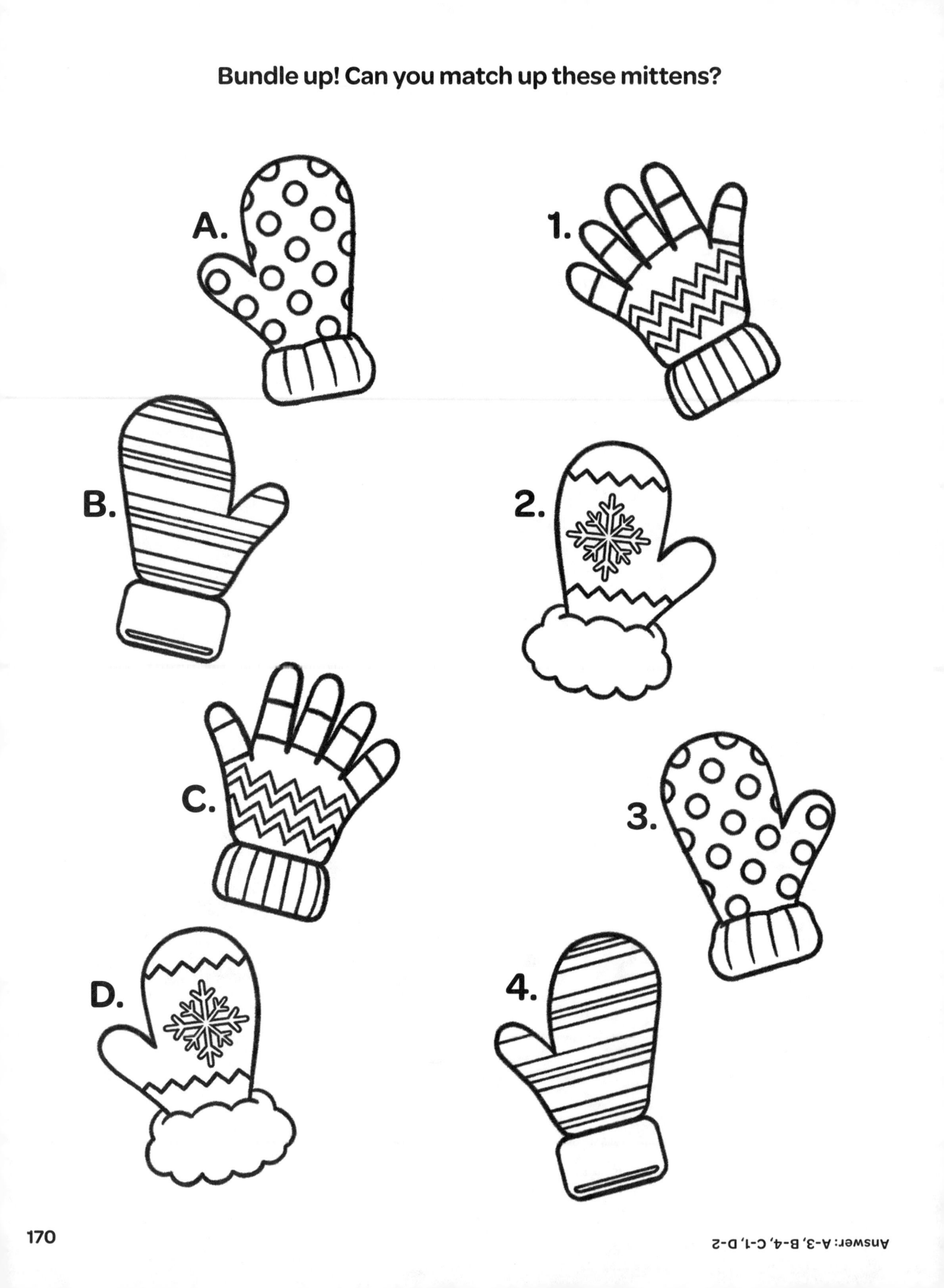


Answer: A-3, B-4, C-1, D-2

What's your favorite type of weather?
Draw it in a scene below!

Fill this red barn with animals!

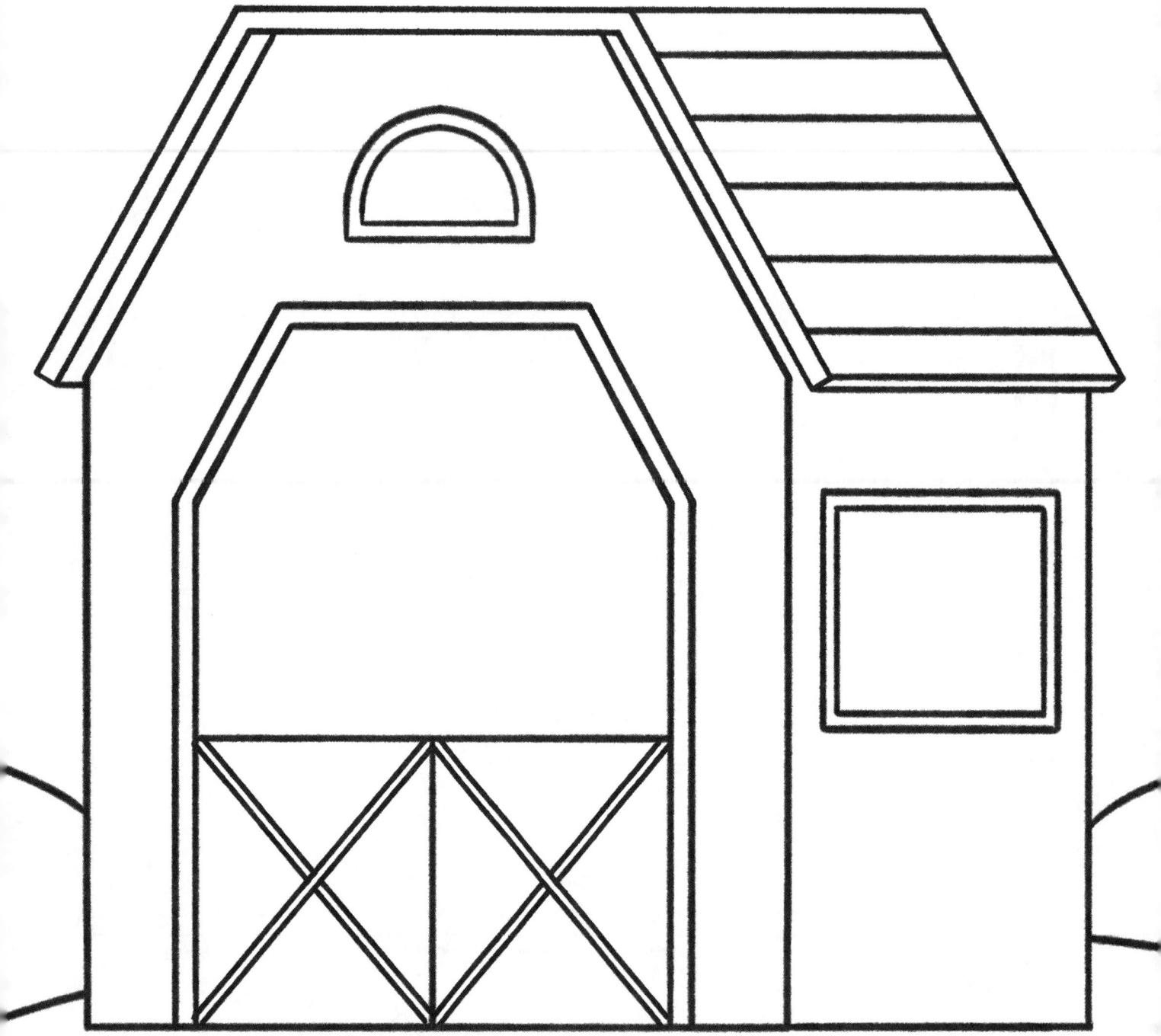

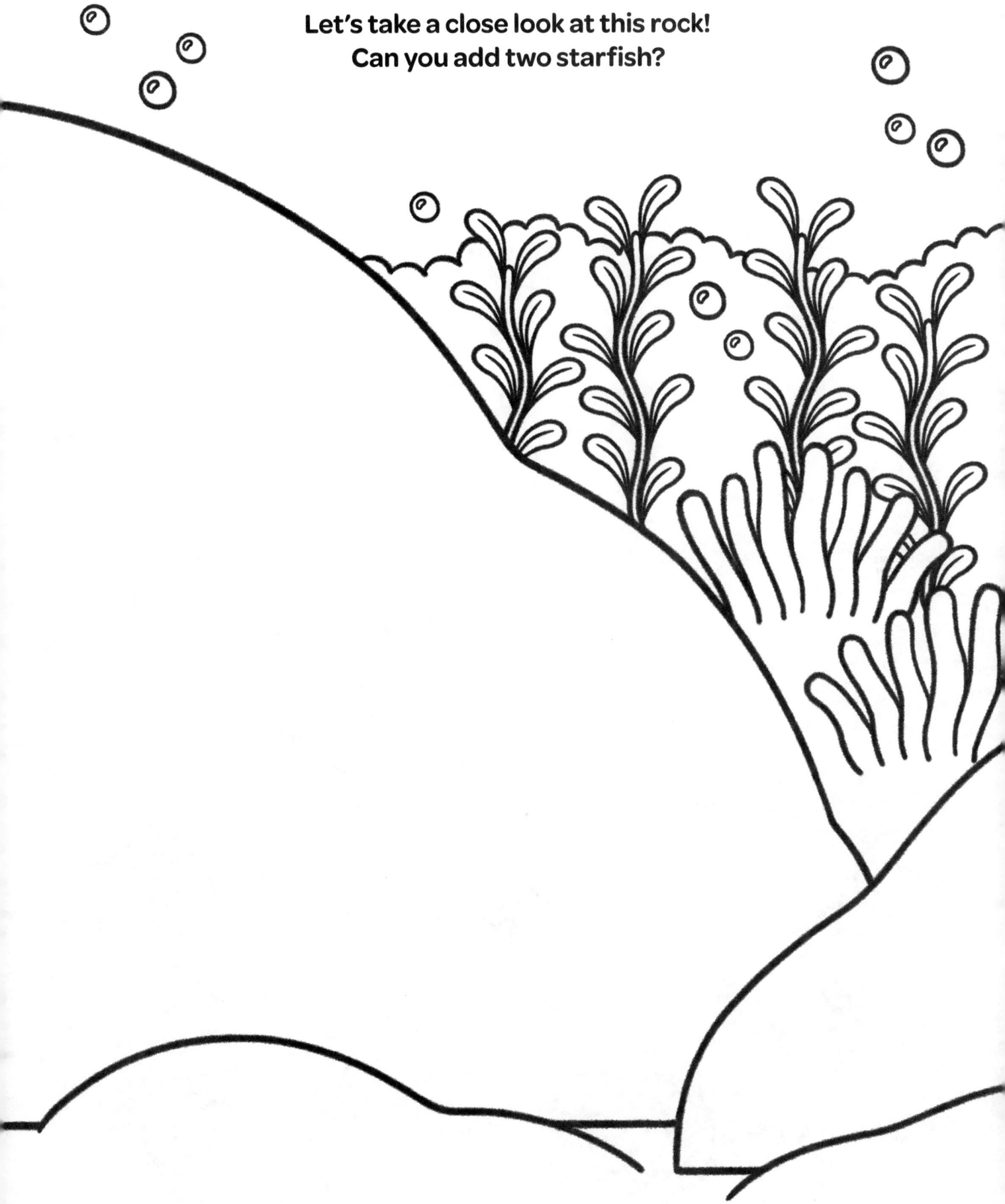

Let's take a close look at this rock!
Can you add two starfish?

**Those are beautiful flowers!**
**Add three butterflies.**

Snails are slow animals!

Match each item to its shape!

CUBE

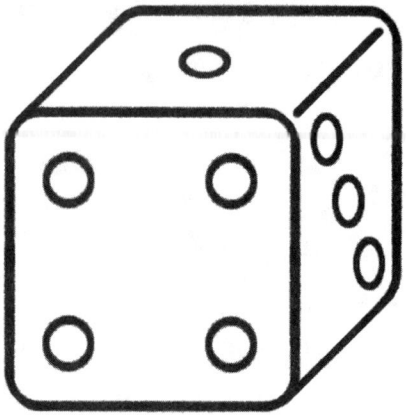

PYRAMID

CYLINDER

Answers on page 192

***Choo! Choo!*** **Pick the path that goes to the train.**

Answer: B

**This animal can hear sounds from a long distance away!**
**Connect the dots to find out what animal this is!**

**Spot the three differences in this scene!**

Answers on page 192

Can you match each meal to its name?

PRETZEL

CHICKEN

BURGER

SALAD



Answers on page 192

**Draw a train chugging along on these tracks!**

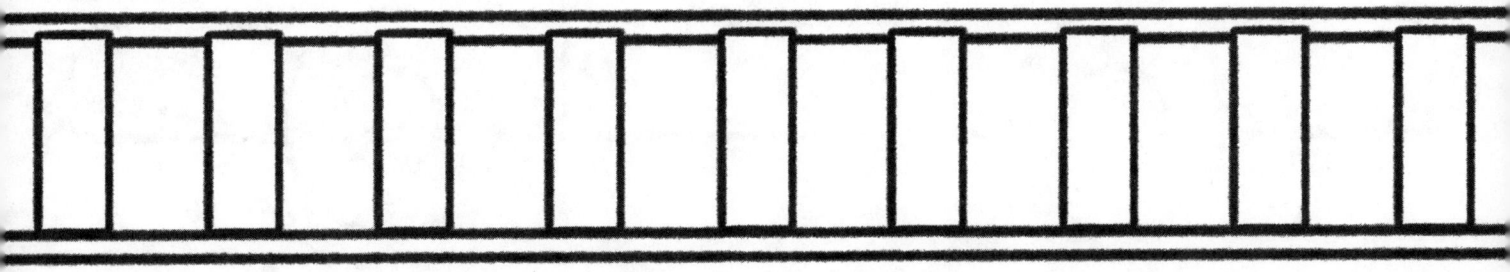

A fire truck quickly gets firefighters to the scene to help people!

**Orcas are often referred to as whales—
but they actually belong to the dolphin family!**

This crab is happy to be on the beach.
Color him in!

**Sunlight helps plants grow!**
**Help the sun's rays find the bed of flowers.**

Answer: B

**Outer space is vast.**
**Design a new planet!**

Spot the three differences in this scene!

Answers on page 192

***Chirp! Chirp!*** **Match the number with the correct group of chicks!**

**3**

**6**

**2**

**5**



Answers on page 192

CERTIFICATE
OF COMPLETION
CONGRATULATIONS
1°

# ANSWERS

Page 4

Page 5

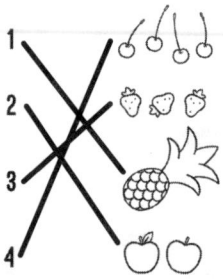


Page 21

Page 22

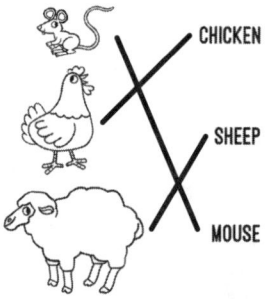


Page 27

Page 29

Page 31

Page 32

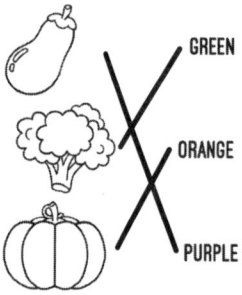


Page 39

Page 41

Page 47

Page 49

Page 51

Page 52

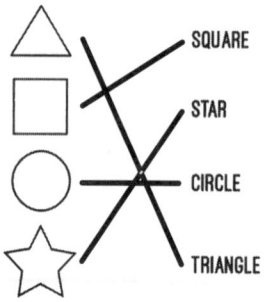


Page 59

Page 61

Page 68

Page 71

Page 81

Page 86

Page 89

Page 91

Page 98

Page 99

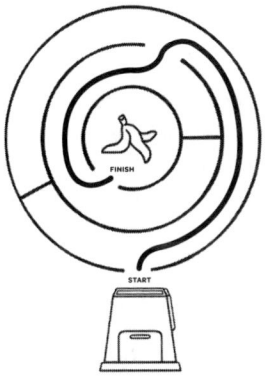


Page 101

Page 109

Page 111

Page 117

Page 118

Page 121

Page 131

Page 139

Page 141

Page 147

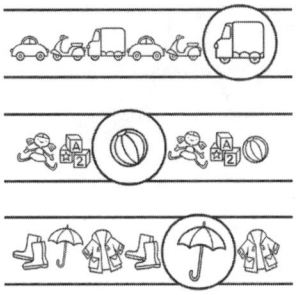

Page 149

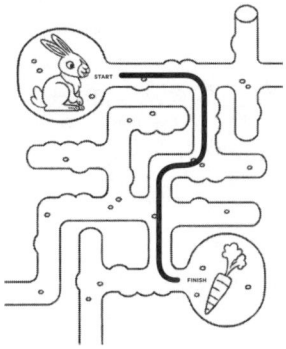


Page 151

Page 152

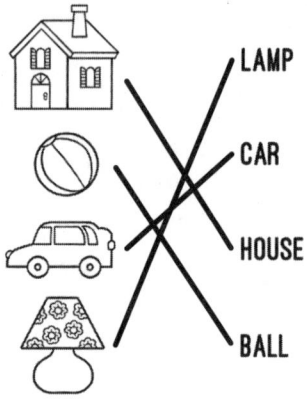


Page 157

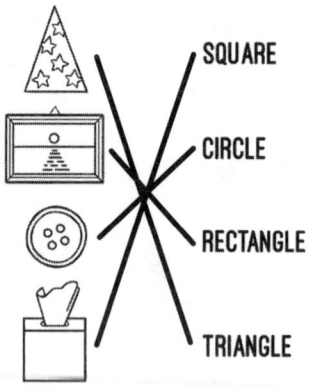


Page 161

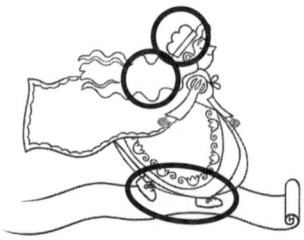

Page 162

Page 166

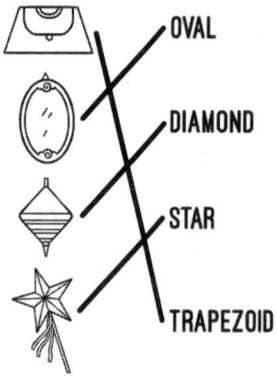


Page 167

Page 169

Page 176

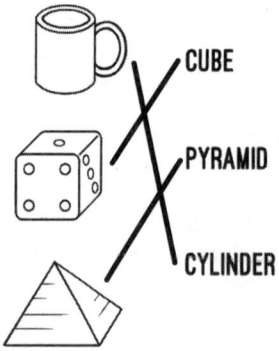


Page 179

Page 180

Page 187

Page 188

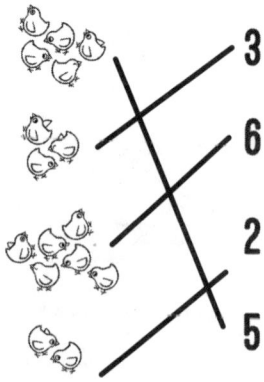